THIS
ISN'T LOVE

THIS
ISN'T LOVE

SUNDAY TIMES BESTSELLING AUTHOR

HOPE DANIELS
WITH ANN CUSACK

MIRROR BOOKS

MIRROR BOOKS

All of the events in this story are true, but some
names and details have been changed to protect the
identities of individuals.

© Hope Daniels

1

Published in Great Britain and Ireland in 2024 by
Mirror Books, a Reach PLC business.

www.mirrorbooks.co.uk
@TheMirrorBooks

Print ISBN 9781915306722
eBook ISBN 9781915306739

Editing and Prodcution: Harri Aston, Christine Costello

Printed and bound in Great Britain by
CPI Group (UK) Ltd, Croydon, CR0 4YY

I dedicate this book to my strong and kind mum – you are finally living in peace and free from abuse.

Author's Note

Thank you most of all for buying this book. I cannot tell you how much it means to me.

In my previous book, *Hackney Child* I skimmed over certain important events in my life, such as my time in foster care. Back then, I didn't even realise I'd been abused. I tried to protect the very people who had hurt me; my foster carers, my abuser. I thought it was my fault, not theirs. Since *Hackney Child* I've had a major breakdown and I've come to terms with all these issues. I've also learned that my mother, whilst she made mistakes, was a victim herself. This book addresses all of this, once and for all. For me, it's closure; it's my full stop. There is no more shame, no more secrets. This is my everything. I hope you can enjoy it – it's a bumpy ride but there is so much light at the end.

Love, Hope x

1

SPORTS DAY, GREATER LONDON, SUMMER 1988

WAFTING THROUGH the window, along with the irresist-ible smell of sausages, was the sound of Duran Duran's *Wild Boys*. I slipped on my trainers with a smile. My favourite food and my favourite band. This was going to be good.

The children's home where I lived had organised a sports day and I just couldn't wait. One last time, I checked myself over in the mirror, frowning at my white shorts with the pocket on the side, my faded Michael Jackson 'Bad' T-shirt and a pair of grubby hand-me-down trainers which probably once were white before they reached me.

You're podgy. Too pale. Legs like corned beef. Oh, girl, you've got a spot on your chin!

Defiantly, I pushed the thoughts away.

Not today, thank you.

Outside, the grounds were already filling up with kids and care workers. Someone was cremating sausages on a barbecue. I'd never even been to a barbecue in all my 14 years! One of the youth workers was setting up a camcorder to film the races. Another was the unofficial DJ, hits blaring from a ghetto blaster.

'The reflex is a lonely child, who's waiting by the park…'

I was in love with Duran Duran, Simon Le Bon specifically, and I had long-term plans to marry him. I knew he was already married, but I also knew marriages didn't last that long.

"Over here, Hope!" called Callum, one of the social workers. "Give me a hand setting up this assault course, would you?"

I ran over, brimming with excitement, thrilled to be called upon. Together, we laid out the course, lining up apples which the contestants would pick up with their mouths. Next, we dragged a large gymnastics horse across the grass, then we laid out skipping ropes. There was an egg and spoon race and a sack race too, plus a running race where we'd have to spin around halfway through and stagger, dizzy and giggly, towards a blurred finish line.

These were races designed, really, for much younger children. But in many ways, we were still babies. Emotionally fragile; raw. I could steal a week's worth of food and look after two children, no problem. But no way could I sit still and listen for 10 minutes. Anyway, it wasn't the races themselves that I was really looking forward to. I wanted to be involved in the planning, the organising, the keeping of scores. What I wanted, most of all, was for someone to ruffle my mousy-brown hair and say:

"Well done, Hope, thanks for your help. We couldn't have managed without you."

More than anything, I needed to be needed.

My mind flashed back to two chubby faces, smudged with kebab sauce, their sticky hands clutching tightly onto mine. A phantom of a memory sliced through me like a knife. I missed them so much.

"Hope, can you run and ask the kitchen for six hard boiled eggs?" Callum asked, breaking my daydream.

I beamed; glad, grateful even, to be of use.

By the time the races began, the place was teeming with relatives, local bigwigs and visiting social workers. The kids were hyped, drunk on the anticipation, screaming, laughing, acting out practice races. For me there was comfort in chaos, a certain safety in mania. It reminded me of the jumble sales and bustling markets where Dad and I used to push and shove our way to the front for bargains.

"You keep 'em talking, Hope, I'll nick as much as I can get my hands on."

Back then, I'd been so proud of my Dad. Sharpest thief I knew. He was like a magician, the way he could disappear a whole bottle of whisky into the unfathomable folds of his black overcoat. He'd taught me all the tricks, all his shoplifting secrets. But I was hoping I wouldn't need them, not when Simon Le Bon came calling for me with his great big pile of money and his fancy car.

The whistle went, and I was busy cheering on my friends in the sack race, when I heard someone calling my name. I turned around and saw Tiffany, a familiar face from the children's home. She was two years older than me, and she'd left a few months earlier to get her own place.

"You alright?" she asked, in an off-hand sort of way.

Truth was, she and I were not pals. She'd been mean to me when I first arrived at the home, shoving me out of the dinner queue, teasing me about my weight. She wasn't the only one;

most of the older girls seemed to take great delight in picking at us younger ones. But I'd faced bigger bullies than them and I'd stood up to Tiffany and the others. They soon learned to leave me alone. But I was wary of her, all the same.

"What are you doing here?" I asked.

"I'm back to watch sports day," she smiled. "Back to watch you all make idiots of yourselves. And I got married, didn't you hear? This is my husband, Dougie."

She slipped her arm around the bloke next to her and winked. I had to admit, I was shell-shocked.

"Married?" I whistled. "Wow! Like, actually married?"

It was as though she'd announced she'd found a cure for cancer, or she'd just come back from climbing Everest. Girls like us, girls from care, just didn't get married. Nobody wanted us. We were dirty and damaged. We were lost, vulnerable, broken. We just were not marriage material.

"Married!" I said again, rolling the word around my mouth, trying it out for size. It felt too big, too important for me, as though I had no right to say it. I wanted to ask Tiffany how she'd done it, how she'd wrangled it, but I couldn't quite manage it. My head swam with visions of her in a sparkling white dress and silver shoes, in the arms of a dashing groom, under the twinkling lights of a beautiful ballroom. I was eaten up with longing – and possibility. If Tiffany could do it, was there a chink of hope for me too? Was there a fairytale ending for me? Tiffany showed me her ring, it was a cheap band, too tight for her finger and leaving a greenish tinge on her skin. But that didn't matter. It was a ring. It was a status symbol. It was where I wanted to be. She was fast becoming a hero in my eyes.

Dougie was not exactly a dashing groom, but it turned out he was quite a laugh. He was anything from early-20s to mid-30s; an old man in my eyes. But he was full of jokes and wisecracks; confident and cocksure.

"Run and get me a hot dog, there's a good girl," he grinned.

He took one bite and tossed it over his shoulder, into a crowd of people. For some reason, I found it funny as the ketchup splattered onto someone's suit. I laughed along with Dougie and Tiffany, and Dougie's mate, Trev.

When it was my turn to race, my good mood suddenly evaporated. I felt so exposed, standing on the start line. It felt more like a firing line. In an instant, I was back to being clumsy and shy and 14 again.

"Good luck, Hope!" Dougie shouted.

If I was hoping for a fairytale, then I was sadly mistaken. I struggled to clamber up onto the gymnastics horse and then felt myself falling from the other side, belly-flopping with a thud onto the ground. There was a ripple of suppressed laughter amongst the crowd, and I buried my face in the grass, my whole body scalded with shame.

"Don't worry," said a voice, standing over me. "Come on, it's just a stupid race."

I looked up to see Dougie holding out his hand. When he pulled me up, he yelled: "Run for your life!" and chased me all the way into the trees at the edge of the grounds. When I tripped, breathless and laughing, he dived on me and tickled me until I yelled for mercy. His fingers ran over my skin like spiders. I felt horribly self-conscious and awkward, but oddly triumphant too. As though I'd snapped a cord, and I was untethered and free.

"See!" he grinned, falling back onto his knees and flicking

grass from his shoulders. "Sports day, that's just kiddie stuff. I've got a much better idea for a bit of fun."

Standing up to brush myself off, I caught Tiffany, glaring at me, her mouth set in a tight line of disapproval.

Serves you right for being a bully. No wonder your husband prefers me.

"So, Friday, the other girls go home for the weekend, and you could use that as an excuse to meet me," Dougie was saying. "Waterloo station, under the clock. You, me, Tiffany and Trev. Few drinks. We'll have a right laugh. What do you think?"

He had it all worked out. I nodded, speechless. I watched Dougie slick back his greasy hair and run his tongue, briefly, across his lips. Repulsed and flattered in equal measure, I nodded again.

That night, whilst everyone else was chatting about sports day, I thought only of Dougie and Tiffany and that shiny band on her ring finger which symbolised everything I'd ever dreamed of.

"Married," I said to myself. "She was in care, and now she's married."

The more I said it, the more I liked it. The more I wanted it to be me. Suddenly, there was hope ahead. The future shimmered with potential. Maybe fairytales did come true, after all.

2

HARTEPOOL, 2016

EVEN THOUGH I'd spoken at quite a few of these conferences, I was gripped by an attack of nerves as I drove north up the motorway. And walking into a packed room, looking out across a sea of more than a hundred faces, professional faces, did nothing to ease my anxiety which crackled like static around the stage. Fidgeting with my notes, mentally rehearsing my lines, I felt like a complete imposter.

I had been asked to speak to representatives from the police, social services, health and education about being a child in care. These were the same professions who'd had full control over my life as I grew up. Now I was here to advise them. It was almost laughable, and it didn't sit right with me at all. To shroud my unsuitability, I'd invested in a new and expensive shift dress. I'd bought a posh pen and a nice leather bag. Who was I trying to kid?

"I'm Hope Daniels," I announced, with a half-attempt at a half-smile.

Covering my transition into care, my speech followed the

familiar path. But then, for some reason, I veered completely off track.

"When I was a teenager, I was numb to relationships," I told them. "I made mistakes. In fact, at 14, I had an affair with an older man. My friend's husband, actually."

The words were sharp and painful on my tongue. My mouth stung. What was I thinking, confessing this, my darkest secret, to a room full of strangers? Hastily, I reshuffled my papers and changed the subject. There was a cold sheen of sweat, like cling film, over my face. I couldn't wait to get out of there. As I stepped down from the podium, one eye on the exit door, a young, dark-haired police officer came over.

"Can I ask you something?" he said. "You mentioned your affair with an older man?"

An electric fence of embarrassment hummed between us.

"Yeah," I muttered awkwardly. "I was a little slag back then, I do apologise."

It was excruciating to verbalise, but I was good at self-criticism. I'd had enough practice over the years, after all.

"No," he said firmly. Fiercely almost. "No. It wasn't an affair. It was child abuse. Have you heard of CSE?"

I shook my head.

"Child Sexual Exploitation," he explained. "You were the victim. Not the perpetrator. There was no affair, Hope. There was no relationship."

I was dumbfounded. Stepping backwards, I sank onto a chair, my papers fluttering to the floor.

"Are you sure?" I hesitated. "Nobody has ever told me this before. It was my fault, I'm sure it was. I knew he was married, and I just went ahead anyway.".

Even now, saying it out loud, my soul burned with a seismic shame.

"It absolutely was not your fault," he assured me. "Nowadays, he'd be arrested, and you'd be taken to a place of safety. I'm only sorry you didn't get the support you needed."

In that moment, my world jolted and shifted. Here I was, at a safeguarding conference, being told I, myself, had not been kept safe. The revelation was enormous. But in that moment, a single atom of the shame and blame which had weighed on me, and bent me double throughout my life, was lifted. From me. To him. This was the start of my healing.

3

HACKNEY, 1983

FUNNILY ENOUGH, just like the sports day at the children's home, it's the smell of my childhood that has lingered with me through the years. But there were no barbeques at our house. No sausages under the grill. We didn't even have a working cooker most of the time, and we certainly didn't have food in the fridge. It stings my nostrils, even now, to remember the overpowering stench of urine, sweat and ground-in filth that seeped out of every brick in every single place we lived. My parents were addicts; their days, their lives, their worlds, revolving around booze. And only booze. Me and my three brothers, one older, two younger, were incidental; bit-part players in our parents' ongoing dramas. Worse than that even, we got in the way.

On the outside, my mum was, through my child's eyes, impossibly glamorous. She wore thick Max Factor make-up, which my father stole to order for her, and her lipstick was always the brightest shade of red. I loved it back then. Now, through the lens of middle-age, I can see it was garish and brash. She wore high stiletto heels and a skirt just an inch or two above her knee. She walked effortlessly in her heels too; she was the sort of woman who could win a race in three-inch heels. Her hair, dyed blonde, was always styled and flicked out defiantly at the ends. Dad, too, was smartly dressed, usually he wore a suit and tie. He shaved daily and applied copious layers of Brylcreem to his hair. I thought they were both such a good-looking pair though my childhood bias, did not, of course, take account of the way they smelled.

In contrast, me and my brothers were badly dressed, and we were filthy. I usually had nits and my shoulder-length light brown hair was matted and knotty. Mum cut it a couple of times at home, so it was jagged at the ends. I had never been to a hairdresser. In photos of that time, I am wearing charity clothes; dresses which are far too big, cardigans which fray over the ends of my fingers. I was a little overweight, for though I was hungry half of the time, the rest of the time I ate junk food and unhealthy rubbish. I was tall too, for my age, and I liked to think it was my body's way of responding to the weight of responsibility which I carried. Like any little girl, I idolised my mother and father. It was only as the months and years passed that the chunks were chipped off their pedestal, until it cracked and broke completely. They did not so much fall from their elevated position, as slowly crumple, into a dusty and disappointing heap.

After I started school, and I met other children and parents, I began to question why Mum had an endless supply of make-up, yet we didn't have soap or shampoo in the bathroom. We didn't even have food in the house. Dad had a good, thick winter coat, but my brothers and I shivered as we walked to school in hand-me-downs from local charities. We had no washing machine but there was always money to buy whisky. It is hard to come to terms with the level of abject neglect we experienced but it is harder still to admit that my parents neglected us more than they neglected themselves. They had their issues with addiction, certainly. But the fact remains that they cared for themselves, and they did not care for us. It was a further twist of the knife, throughout those long, lonely years of my childhood. And it is the aspect I find most difficult of all to forgive.

From birth, me and my siblings were on the 'at risk' register and sometimes I saw more of our social worker than I did of my own mother. We were known to each agency that had a name, and yet somehow, absurdly, we slipped through every net. Me and my family were regularly evicted from houses, B&Bs and hostels, tramping around Hackney and Bethnal Green, never staying for long, never putting down roots. We might just have settled in at a new school when, no explanation, no apology, we were off again, trundling down the road pushing an old pram stuffed with our belongings, with insults from angry neighbours smacking our retreating heads like pebbles.

"Good riddance! Time they took those kids into care! You don't deserve them!"

Yet no matter how many times we moved, how far we tried to run, the bad smell came with us. And as the years passed, I began to suspect that the smell came from inside of us. It came from within.

* * * *

A lie-in was never an option. For a start, I was nine years old, full to the brim with energy and enthusiasm. More pressingly, my wet nightie was sticking to my legs and the damp patch on the mattress was cold and unfriendly. Bed was not a place I wanted to be. Skipping downstairs, expertly avoiding the nails and carpet tacks on the bare boards, I checked the kitchen cupboards. Empty, obviously. Well girl, it was worth a try.

"Hope! Hope! I'm starving! What's for breakfast?"

My little brothers Harold, six, and Jack, five, bounded down the stairs, faces open and expectant, bellies rumbling.

"Don't worry," I smiled. "I've got something in mind. Won't be long."

It was my job to feed them. Just as it was my job to bath them and tuck them into bed each night. I was a child raising children, a little mother even though I was myself practically motherless. Yet there was no resentment, no sense of crushing responsibility. I loved looking after my brothers, seeing their eyes light up when I came home with a family bag of crisps and a packet of custard creams. I needed to be loved. I needed a reason to be. And they offered me both.

"You two cuddle up on the couch," I told them, flicking on the telly Dad had found in a skip some months earlier. There was only one working channel, but it was better than nothing.

Pulling on the least filthy pair of jeans I could find, I grabbed a sweatshirt and disappeared out of the door. Even at nine, I considered myself an accomplished shoplifter. Dad had taught me all his tricks, taking me out to watch him at work ever since I was knee high. And what a show it was. I felt privileged to be in the presence of a true wizard.

"Wow!" I breathed, open mouthed, as he helped himself to a big bag of sherbet lemons from a market stall.

Dad had a big coat with bottomless pockets, and I believed

he could stash unlimited booty in there. That coat was a Tardis, woven in black.

"The 'up the sleeve' trick is a good one," he told me conspiratorially. "Or you can fake illness, tell 'em you're going to throw up, cause a distraction. Go for sympathy, or pity maybe. Nobody's gonna challenge a kid, especially not you with your pretty face."

I swelled with pride. I felt honoured to be a partner in crime, privy to state secrets. This was the Hackney version of entry into the magic circle, and I treated it with the reverence and solemnity it deserved.

"If all else fails, just grab and scarper," Dad added. "Snatch whatever you fancy and run for your life."

So, whilst other kids were working hard to pass a maths exam, or to learn piano Grade Four, I was concentrating on becoming an accomplished thief. Dad and I trawled the markets on Bethnal Green's Roman Road and Ridley Road in Hackney, and I honed my skills. And it turned out I had quite a talent for it; nipping under market stalls, round the back of shelves, through the legs of other customers. I rarely got caught, and even if I did, who would punish a child?

"You're good at this," Dad said approvingly. "Must run in the family."

Shoplifting was, to me, an art form and I was proud of my ability. In class, when the teacher asked us what we wanted to be when we grew up, my first thought was 'thief'. I had flair and expertise. I had spirit, and I had bags and bags of cheek. I didn't once feel bad about breaking the law. I was stealing from the rich to feed the poor, to feed my own little brothers. I loved the tale of Robin Hood and I liked to see myself as the Maid

Marian of Hackney. In essence, in the great scheme of things, I was helping to balance social injustice – aged nine!

On this particular morning, with Harold and Jack needing breakfast, I felt supremely confident I could deliver. I even relished the challenge. There was always that heart-stopping moment as my hand reached out for the prize, and my stomach dropped, simultaneously, right through my feet. Yet the fear was all part of the fun. I'd decided to run down the high street to nick whatever breakfast I could find and, as I turned the corner, I spotted a greengrocer laying out a box of shiny red apples.

They're crying out to be nicked!

I sauntered along, cool as you like, remembering everything Dad had told me. I let myself walk a half-step past the apples, before reaching back, lighting fast, and making the grab. But just not fast enough.

"Hey!" shouted the greengrocer, dashing out from behind his counter.

My mistake was to try to grab two apples in one hand; my palms just weren't big enough, and as I dropped one, I faltered. It was a fatal hesitation. I set off running, just one apple in each hand, my basic maths unable to work out how they would divide between the three of us.

"Where do you think you're going, young lady?" asked a voice, more bemused than annoyed.

I was yanked back by my sweatshirt, and it was time for trick number two. If you can't outrun them, charm them instead.

"Gordon Bennett, Mister! Mind the cloth please. This isn't my sweatshirt, you know."

"I suppose you stole that as well?" he asked.

I looked suitably offended and, as I saw a smile puckering, I knew I'd won. Hooked like a haddock. Time for trick number three. The sympathy vote.

"Me and my little brothers, we've got no breakfast," I told him. "Gordon Bennett, I'm sorry about your apples, I really am. But we're so hungry. Look at me, look mister, can't you see I'm starving?"

Minutes later, I was leaving the shop with three apples, three pears and a punnet of plums.

"And next time, you ask before you take!" he shouted, as I ran off down the street.

"Gordon Bennett! I promise I will!" I replied, my mouth already stuffed with plum.

Marching home, I congratulated myself on my stealing prowess; I couldn't wait to tell Dad all about it. A real chip off the old block. It's only now, looking back, I realise most of the shopkeepers probably knew full well what I was up to, and they turned a blind eye. I didn't need to fake illness or make people laugh. I just needed to tell the truth.

It was as I was pausing to wipe rivulets of juice from my chin that I heard a faint whine from a nearby bin. There it was again. I sauntered over, and to my astonishment, I saw a bag, wriggling and mewling, dumped in the bin with all the rubbish. Peering back at me were three, wide-eyed, bedraggled kittens. I felt a rush of maternal outrage. Who on earth would do a thing like this? Who would abandon three helpless babies? I could have asked my own parents the same question, but I might have got a more sensible answer from the mother cat.

"Don't worry," I whispered, pulling the bag open further and peering inside. "I'm here now."

Scooping it up, I somehow made it home with three crying

kittens, three apples, three pears and an almost-full punnet of plums. There was no sign of my mother, and Dad was out cold, so I hid the kittens under my bed, and instructed them to be quiet.

"After I've had my apple, I'll nip out and see if I can find a pint of milk for you three," I told them. "Quiet mind, or you'll get thrown out. Nobody lasts long around here if they make a fuss."

Those black and white kittens weren't my only rescue project. I once found a stray cat which later gave birth under my bed. The house was overrun with tabby kittens. Another time, I brought home a pigeon with a broken wing. I couldn't resist a sob story, as much for my sake as theirs. It was wonderful to feel someone, or something, was relying upon me. I especially loved to cuddle my kittens in bed with me. It was the only sort of affection I ever got. But as soon as my mother discovered my pets, she chased them from the bedroom and slung them back onto the street.

"I can't feed you kids, never mind about a bloody cat," she complained.

It broke my heart each time I lost a pet. All through my childhood, I vowed to have a whole menagerie of animals as soon as I had my own place. Yet sadly, as an adult, the idea of having a pet in my home – the mess, the smell, the noise – is too overwhelming for me. It is too sharp a reminder of the childhood I am desperate to leave behind.

4

IT WAS way past midnight when the bedroom door opened and my mother fell clumsily against the bed frame, swearing loudly through the darkness. If I'd been asleep, I certainly wouldn't be now, I thought grumpily. Truth was, I was wide awake, I'd been waiting for this, dreading it. The man behind her; short and portly, with more hair up his nose than on his head, flicked on the bedside light and instantly his gaze settled on me. I stared back, more defiant, more combative, than I really felt. The fumbling began, along with the noises, and I cringed. Much as I loathed it, much as I abhorred what was happening, I was also transfixed. And then, the part I hated the most, where Mum's moaning transmogrified into a howl; like a wounded animal, crying out in pain and protest.

"Stop!" I yelled, springing upright in bed. "Stop it! You're hurting her!"

The man ignored me. My bed was facing theirs and so all I got in reply was the sight of his fat, white buttocks pumping up and down and wobbling like a great vanilla blancmange. I dug my fingers into my palms sharply enough for the pain to distract me. But it didn't work, and Mum cried out again.

"Stop!" I screamed.

The man paused and peered at me from over his shoulder.

"Shut up you little slag," he hissed. "You want it instead? You whore. You fucking slut. Do you want some? Do you?"

He jutted his chin out towards me, and I shrank back with a shiver. I didn't cry out again. Instead, I repeated the mantra in my head: 'You are a little slag. You are a little whore. You are a little slut.' I felt the bed grow warm, and then horribly cold, as, in sheer terror, I wet myself. The man, by now, was squashing his hairy belly into his trousers, ready to belt up and leave. He slapped a fiver onto the bedside table with no more than a cursory glance at my mother. To me, as he left, he said: "Remember that kiddo, it's your turn next time if you don't shut the fuck up."

I kept my gaze fixed on the far wall.

'You are a little slag,' I told myself silently. 'You are a little slut. You are a little whore.'

* * * *

Sharing a bedroom with my parents, and therefore with all the punters Mum brought home, was arguably the very worst aspect of my appalling home life. I hated the men, I hated the noises, I hated the smells. Most of all, I hated my mum for letting it all happen. But from an adult's perspective, what disturbs and rattles me most is why my bed was in the same room as theirs in the first place? Why did I have to share a room with the endless stream of punters who crawled up and down our stairs like slugs?

We moved around a lot but mainly we had three-bedroom homes. My older brother, Philip, 20, had one room, and Jack and Harold had another. I shared the third with my parents. Why was that? Why could I not share with my brothers, or even sleep on the sofa? More to the point, why did my mother have to bring her punters into my bedroom? It sickens me now to think that I was maybe somehow part of the package; an unwitting accomplice in Mum's work as a prostitute. Was I a special request? An extra? Looking back, I don't recall Mum ever telling me to be in the bedroom, or even noticing me. I think she was probably too drunk. But I do remember none of the men ever objected to me being there. What kind of man, even a man paying for sex, does so in a house with three young children inside, and a small girl in the room itself?

One of my most disturbing memories is of me locking eyes with the men, from my bed to theirs, and the silence between us, heavy and sticky, spoke volumes. The greedy way they looked at me frightened me as a child, but as an adult, it turns my stomach in pure revulsion. Any objections I raised the following day, any attempts to fight back, were met always with furious indignation by my mother.

"Stay out of it you little bitch!" she screamed. "We need the money."

My father, smiling benignly, poured himself another beaker of whisky, and added, "Do as she tells you, Hope, there's a good girl."

And so, I was trapped. Night after night, I watched and heard different men having sex with my mother, whilst my father either waited downstairs like a spare part or went to the pub to drink away her wages. There were two men, brothers, who visited my mum, who would for some perverted reason pinch her hard, on the chest, whenever the fancy took them. Outraged, I steamed in like a tiny terrier to defend her, snapping and biting at their legs, my small fists balled up and flying.

"Stop it!" my mother yelled, whacking me hard across the back of the head.

They were her pay-packet, her booze-ticket, and sadly I grew to understand she valued that so much more than she valued me. In her drunken rantings, I had heard her wailing about two babies – both girls – who she had been forced to give up for adoption, before I was born. I wondered, in my child's way, whether this was why she resented me so much. Was I a living, unwelcome reminder of the two daughters she had lost? Was my life all about punishment for something which was nothing to do with me? Or was it simply that her brain was so soaked in alcohol that she failed to grasp her grotesque failure in allowing me to witness what went on in that bedroom. She was diagnosed with Wernicke-Korsakoff syndrome or 'wet brain' – a brain disorder linked to heavy drinking – whilst I was still at primary school.

When I first heard the term, I automatically thought of my own wet bed. Wet brain and wet bed. I knew it had to be more than a coincidence, and of course, it was. The two conditions were inextricably and tragically linked, though I didn't quite see how at that age. There was no doubt, however, that alcohol ruled my mother physically, mentally and emotionally.

Growing up, I saw men in two distinct categories: 'Punter/ Not Punter.' It was crass and it was base, but this was how I had been conditioned, right from being a toddler. Men, to me, were about sex, and nothing else. I had learned, because I'd had to learn, how to distinguish between those who would likely pay for sex and those who would not. And practice had made me just about perfect.

One of mum's clients was a smartly dressed man named Albert. He was a long-term customer, calling in every week or so right through my childhood and even after I'd grown up myself. Albert wore a suit and carried a smart black briefcase, and I was at first in awe of him, thinking he must be some big shot in the city. An oil baron maybe, or a CEO. Maybe, even, he was Prime Minister. Albert didn't swear like all the others, he was softly spoken, and he had small eyes and a weak chin which had almost completely receded into his neck. But just like the others, Albert liked to have me there, in the bedroom, whilst he was having sex with my mum. He'd pause and check over his shoulder, to make sure I was awake and watching. And on his way out, in the half-light, he pressed a hard, shiny coin into my hand.

"Good girl, Hope," he whispered breathlessly. "You're such a good girl."

His voice, so tender, almost girlish, unsettled me much more than the shouting and yelling I was used to. And though the money felt cold in my palm, I felt a thrill of anticipation, as I tried to make out the value of the coin through the gloom. Money! My own money! 50p! I could buy sweets for Harold and Jack. For me too. I could get us a bottle of lemonade! A bag of crisps!

"Salt and vinegar," I murmured to myself. "Yummy!"

Despite the wet bed, I floated off to sleep, the coin growing warm and sticky in my hand. I was really pleased. Later though, I would look back and see the money as payment; was I a sex-worker, I asked myself, just like my mother? Was I just as bad as she was? It was hush money, it was blackmail, thirty pieces of silver to buy my silence, or buy my presence. The guilt washed through me, and it left a lasting stain on my soul.

I am a whore. I am a little slag. I am a slut.

5

OVER THE summer of 1983, just after my ninth birthday, all the bad stuff in my life grew inexplicably worse. There was less food, less money, more arguments. Even the smell got worse. We'd had two trips to hospital too. I'd been bitten by the neighbour's dog, just above my ankle, and when I limped home, screaming and sobbing, Mum came rushing downstairs, half dressed and spitting in annoyance. She was followed by a man I didn't recognise.

"You silly little cow!" she shouted. "What' ya get yourself bitten for?"

My leg was bleeding, dripping into my shoe, and the strange man said, "She needs to get that checked. Look, I've got my car outside, I'll take you both."

I was revolted by the idea of getting into a car with one of Mum's punters. And for him to be the one to take me to hospital, well, that seemed like a sick joke. I was disgusted, by him, and by my mother. But I had no choice. I wrapped my leg in an old tea towel and limped outside, into the back seat. I didn't get to go in cars much, but I was determined not to be impressed or show any enjoyment whatsoever, and I set my mouth in a firm straight line. At the hospital, we booked in, and the receptionist smiled and said, "You go and sit down over there with your Daddy, love."

I swore under my breath at her. It wasn't long before my leg was cleaned and dressed, and it turned out the wound was not particularly serious. What upset me far more than the pain was the way the doctors assumed Mum and her punter were my parents. I felt all scrunched up with anger, desperate to stand on one of the plastic hospital chairs and yell the truth from the bottom of my lungs. But I was unable to find the words. I knew he'd been having sex with my mother, but only because I'd heard it said. I didn't actually understand what sex was. And I thought that everyone paid for it. It was a business transaction, a bit like buying a cat or a dog maybe but with all that mess and the bottomless feeling of shame.

After our spell in A&E, the man said to me, "Come on, I'll buy you a burger for being a good girl. There's a McDonald's down the street."

I stared hard at him and said nothing. But I was in turmoil inside. On the one hand, I wanted nothing from this filthy man. I hated him. Yet I had never in my life had a cheeseburger. I'd never once been to McDonald's. Minutes later, as I held my first cheeseburger in my hand, my head swam with conflicting voices. I felt like a traitor for enjoying the burger, yet I just couldn't help myself. As a compromise, I waited until I'd finished the last mouthful, and then instead of saying 'thank you' to the man, I told him: "Fuck off." To me, that was redressing the balance a little, showing I hadn't sold out completely, and it was the best I could do. The bite healed quickly but the following week, we were playing in the garden when our neighbours began lopping rocks and bricks over the fence. It wasn't particularly unusual; we were not a popular family. Jack didn't duck in time and a half brick caught him on the side of the head and gashed his skull. There was blood everywhere.

"Ow!" he yelled. "Ow! Hope!"

That was the thing: If they were hurt, or hungry, or afraid, my little brothers did not shout for their mother or even their father. They shouted for me. That afternoon, Mum and Dad were in the pub, and so Philip and I took Jack, on the bus, to hospital. His head had to be stitched and bandaged and I sat with him throughout and held his hand. Nobody questioned why a nine-year-old girl was in charge. Nobody asked Philip or I where our parents were.

We were scruffy and unwashed and, of course, we stank. Yet it raised no alarm bells. Much of the time, the neglect was mistaken for poverty, I think, and poverty is much simpler to resolve than neglect. People thought they could help by giving us a free meal or donating a pair of shoes. But that was merely a sticking plaster. There was enough money passing through our home, the problem was, we never saw a penny of it. And so at the hospital, just as on so many other occasions, the chance to save us was missed.

Because it was the school summer holidays, we didn't have any structure or support. At school, there was a lovely lady in the office called Diane who had a bag of spare clothes for me to root through and borrow. She'd let me wear whatever I wanted and then give it back to her to wash and dry ready for the next time. I loved the school library too; I'd curl up in a corner and read all the fairytales; Cinderella, Snow White, Sleeping Beauty. I loved to lose myself in worlds of magic and make-believe. Even the scary fairytales – the lands of wicked stepmothers, giants and wolves dressed as grannies – well, that was nothing compared to my real life. But my favourites were the happy endings, always.

'And so, the prince and princess lived happily ever after,' I read, closing my book with a warm, wistful feeling. One day, that might be me. It just might.

In term-time, we got free school meals, milk and snacks, and my teachers did their best to look after us. Our headteacher was cuddly, like a big pillow, and she had a wide, open smile. Each day, before we went home, she wrapped her arms around me and, with my face lost in the pleats of her dress, I felt the warmth of her affection and care.

"You're not on your own, Hope," she'd tell me. "I'm here for you. Please don't forget that."

I relied on that daily reassurance, probably more than I knew, and so the summer holidays, without my teachers, my books, and my snacks, felt very lonely. Hackney was an area with pockets of terrible deprivation, and local charities and support groups offered free food and holiday projects, for kids like me. I grew good at finding those places, to make sure me and my brothers didn't starve.

I was stealing more too during that holiday, priding myself on picking up a sausage roll, a loaf of bread, or a bottle of orange squash. Again, I thought I was a master criminal, but, as before, I think the stallholders knew exactly what I was up to. They saw the dirty clothes, the hair hacked off with blunt scissors, the trainers two sizes too big. And then, of course, there was the smell. Who could possibly fail to notice the smell? Probably, they enjoyed my crime sprees just as much as I did. And if I hadn't tried to steal food, they might well have given it to me for free.

That summer, we'd had an especially hot spell, and the house stank. The bedrooms reeked of soaked-in urine, the toilet wasn't flushing and there was shit encrusted all around the bowl and on the bathroom walls. Each time someone was sick on our carpet, or there was a spillage, Dad simply went out and nicked another roll of carpet, to place on top of the soiled one. Carpet was so easy to steal, there was a local shop with rolls lined up on the pavement, and all Dad had to do was help himself. The carpet didn't quite fit inside his magic coat of course, but he got away with it, regardless. However, squashing the smell of the old carpet underneath a new one served only to make it more pungent. There was often a trickle of brown liquid, of indeterminate origin, leaking out from the layers. We had a family of rats nesting in there too at one point. And so, as the layers of carpets mounted, higher and higher, so did the stink. And with it, our problems.

A couple of weeks earlier, Mum had been sent to prison for soliciting and Dad moped around the house, lost and aimless without her, and more often than not, paralytically drunk. Though he was equally to blame for her arrest, working as her pimp, he didn't take any responsibility, and any regret he showed was only for himself. One August evening, feeling wearier and more weighed down than ever, I had scavenged a local market stall and brought home some bread rolls and a tin of beans for Harold and Jack. I couldn't find a tin opener, and we'd eventually stabbed a hole in the lid with a knife, before eating the beans cold. The boys complained, but it was the best I could do. Mum was still in jail, Dad was in the pub, flushing out his sorrows with neat whisky, and my older brother was with his friends. It was a warm night, and we were playing in the living room, with the windows open, when I heard a low hum of voices outside, growing steadily louder, like the approaching beat of an army.

"What's that, Hope?" asked Harold.

Hurrying to the door, I peered out and saw a gang of our neighbours outside. Even from the doorway, I could feel the anger, bristling like electricity, and just in time, I slammed the door shut before something bounced off the living room window. Three more attempts, and it smashed, bringing a shower of shattered glass down onto the sofa. Each shard glinted and twinkled like a diamond, and I thought immediately of Cinderella and her glass slipper. This, however, was no fairytale. For a few moments, the boys and I were quite still, like cornered animals, afraid even to breathe.

"Upstairs quickly," I whispered. "Don't make a sound, you'll be safe there."

I shut their bedroom door and took up position on the carpetless stairs, feeling, as the oldest family member, aged nine, I had a duty to stand firm. Yet I was completely powerless. They were all adults out there; an angry, baying mob, like hunting dogs, ready to rip me limb from limb. One window after another smashed, and I heard heavy boots kicking at the door.

"Get out! You're a slag, you're not wanted here!"

How did they know? I asked myself helplessly. How did they know, just like Mum's punters knew, that I was a slag and a slut and a whore? There was a whooshing in my ears, like I was underwater, but it wasn't loud enough to drown out the voices. I squeezed my eyes shut tight, and in my mind, I was twirling and whirling around a dance floor, with my handsome prince at my side. As they hammered on the door, I felt a gush around my legs. I had wet myself again. In years to come, I'd learn this was a typical trauma response. Back then, I felt dirty, ashamed and smelly. Long after they had gone, I sat on the stairs, statue still, willing my legs to work, but unable to move. Eventually, hours later, Philip came home and seeing the smashed glass and broken panels, he sighed in sad exasperation.

"Here, help me drag the sofa across the door," he said. "We'll be safe at least."

I went to bed, but I didn't sleep at all. It was cold, with all the windows smashed, and my bed was still wet from the previous night. In the early hours, I heard Dad swearing and shouting, falling over the sofa and yelling out in drunken protest. I got up and began sweeping the glass away. Dad slumped to the floor, splattered with his own vomit and faeces, and began weeping quietly. Just this once, I really wanted him to look after me. Just this once, I really, desperately, needed to be a child.

'I cannot do this any longer,' I told myself. 'I just cannot do it.'

A few hours later, the boys were awake, hungry, grumpy and dismayed by the state of our smashed-up home. Outside, on the blue front door, someone had spray-painted: 'SLAG' in red paint. Again, I thought it must be aimed at me. Again, I had that sensation of my head slipping below water. I was gulping in big mouthfuls and my lungs were about to burst. I reminded myself I had my brothers to think of. As well as a responsibility, they were a much-loved distraction for me too.

"Come on," I said brightly. "We're going swimming."

I knew a back way into the Elephant and Castle swimming baths, avoiding the pay desk. We jumped on a bus for free, and the swim, at least, left us feeling clean and fresh. But putting on our filthy clothes once again was a brutal reminder nothing had changed, and this was a temporary diversion, nothing more. On the bus journey home, we slowed at the traffic lights, and I looked out and saw Stoke Newington police station. Suddenly, I knew what had to be done. Jumping off the bus, with a small, trusting hand in each of mine, I walked straight into the station.

"I need to see my social worker," I said, in the most grown-up voice I could muster. "I'm not going home."

* * * *

And so, in August 1983, along with my brothers, I found myself in a children's home, where I would remain for the next three and a half years. It was clean, warm and, best of all, there was plenty of food – and such a variety on offer too. Cornflakes were a revelation. Yoghurts were a startling new invention. One day, I was given corned beef salad for my tea, and it was the best thing I'd ever tasted.

"Corned beef," I grinned. "Gordon Bennett, I love it."

It became my favourite meal of all time. I'd had no idea such delicacies existed. All through my childhood, I'd clung to the storybook ending of a happy home, a garden, a clean bed and a fridge full of food. And now, I dared to believe, I allowed myself to hope, because it was taking shape, like a mirage, right before my eyes. For the first nine years of my life, food had been so scarce, I'd had to steal it. And whatever I got had to be made to last, because I was never sure where the next meal might come from. In the children's home then, with food available on request, I might have hoped my tangled relationship with food could improve. Instead, it became even more fractured and damaged. Now, though I had plenty of food, I had too much.

It was just too easy. Everyone took it for granted, and it blew my mind. I ate every meal quickly, greedily, as though I was on a timer. I never used a knife and fork, and I hoarded left-overs, and hid them in my room, just in case I ever ran out again. I pinched biscuits and cakes from the larder and stored them away, like a little squirrel, ready for the start of the winter. This was the birth of a lifelong and twisted obsession with food; I'd gone from famine to feast, from starving to satiated, and neither was particularly healthy. I could find no balance.

"Hope, just take your time with your breakfast," the staff urged me. "You can have as many cornflakes as you like. Nobody's going to take them away."

But I didn't believe them. I'd eat with my fingers, one hand gripping tightly onto the bowl, the other scooping cornflakes savagely into my mouth. I was so used to adults telling me lies, I was automatically suspicious of everyone. It took months before I finally started to relax and believe that these changes in my life were here to stay. I didn't have to steal food any longer. I'd never have to steal again! I didn't have to worry about Jack and Harold, they had plenty of food too. I wasn't needed to bath or dress them either.

"You're not their mother," the staff reminded me. "It's our job to look after them. Not yours."

I felt a little pushed out at first. They were my brothers, after all. Yet I also grew to enjoy playing out with the other girls my age. I liked dancing and I loved crafts. I enjoyed just being a little girl, for the first time in my life. I had clean clothes, I even got fresh bed sheets. My hair was washed, I didn't get nits any longer. I wore shoes which fit. It really was like a fairytale come true. If I'd been a character in a Hans Christian Andersen book, my transformation could not have been more complete. My parents were allowed to visit, but were usually drunk and Mum caused trouble, with me, my father, the staff, or all of us at once. She made it clear she came to see my brothers; not me. I was to blame for us going into care, she told me. And so, I blamed myself too.

"You're a grass, Hope," she hissed, her sour whisky breath making my eyes sting. "This is all your fault. You're living it up in this big fancy home, you've no idea what shit I have to put up with."

I didn't like seeing her. And yet I couldn't not see her. I gulped down her criticisms and I beat myself up with her accusations and her insults. She was right. This was all my fault. How could I love myself when my own mother did not love me? Was I somehow so tainted and infected that I actually repelled my mother, the one person who was supposed to love me unconditionally? Dad, as usual, was largely ineffectual. He was pleased to see me, and he did not shout at me. But neither did he stand up for me.

"You've made your bed now, Hope," my mother told me viciously. "You've split your own family right down the middle. Well, you're never coming home. Remember that."

When they visited, I would either wet myself, run away, or freeze completely. These, I would later learn, were my three favoured responses to trauma, and I had no control at all over which one I displayed. Sometimes, I'd run and run. Past the end of the street, through the park, down to the river. I only ever went back when I was caught by a staff member, or maybe a policeman. Wetting myself was the most embarrassing, in terms of how other people saw me, especially as I grew older.

But for me, the most shameful of all, was to do nothing. To be rooted to the spot, like a statue. On these occasions, I felt like a coward and a quitter. It was my job to speak up, my job to look after my brothers, my job to rescue stray cats. And when I failed to do so, I felt wretched. It was my fault. Again.

"None of this is your responsibility, Hope," the youth workers told me. "You need to stop worrying so much. Just enjoy living here."

And in many ways, I did appreciate it. I loved the reliable Monday to Friday routine of breakfast, school, homework, play and bed. I'd never had such regularity in my life before, and I relished it. I began to look forward to Christmas and birthdays too. Back at home, I'd dreaded those dates, not because there was no celebration, but because there was too much. The unpredictability was what I hated the most. Small children need reassurance and routine, and we had a complete absence of both. Each birthday was an excuse for my parents to drink even more than usual and invite all their drunken friends round too. But there was no joy, no fun on these occasions. Mostly, they ended in fights, with what little furniture we had smashed to bits. I don't ever remember hearing my parents actually laugh; I can't imagine how that would sound. My mother cackled, certainly. My father forced a throaty wheeze. But they were not happy, and they did not laugh.

And so a quiet, measured celebration at the children's home was perfect for me. One present. One cake. One card. Less was more. It was wonderful. At nine years of age, I had overdosed on excess and drama, and I was sick of it. It became my goal, even as a child, to smash the mould my parents had built for me. I was determined to be happy; genuinely happy. Growing up, I set myself two rules; not to be like my mother, and not to be a sex worker. Though I didn't fully understand what a sex worker was, I knew enough to realise it was abhorrent. At the children's home, I wanted, so badly, to align myself with this new world of cornflakes and yoghurts, of freshly ironed clothes and polite adults. Yet a part of me hung back, unwilling, or unable, to leave my past behind. At heart, I reminded myself, I was a street urchin, and I was a menace. I was a problem. I was infected, I was a little whore, a little slut, a little slag. And so at nighttime, in the clean, quiet, ordered stillness of the children's home, my heart hammered with panic and the blood pumped loudly in my ears. I did not belong at home. And I did not belong here. Like an animal, raised in captivity, I had been set free, into the wild, but I could not cope with it. In the children's home, I had been thrown a life-ring. I was on a raft. I had lots of support. Yet still, I felt out of my depth. Still, I felt I was drowning.

6

DESPITE MY dysfunctional relationship with my parents, for the first 16 months in care, I was happier than I'd ever remembered. I settled into a routine, I made friends, and I went to school each day. My teacher, Marie, was young and pretty, with pale skin and a rose-bud mouth, features synonymous with my fairytale heroines, Snow White, Cinderella and Belle. I warmed to her immediately. She was gentle and kind too and seemed to see only the good in me, which was a striking change from most of the other adults I'd ever encountered.

"You're a clever girl, Hope," she told me. "Keep working hard at school and you will go far."

I had a notion, even then, I'd like to go to university, but it seemed just as likely that I might go to the moon. Even so, I grew to love Marie and her belief in me meant so much. When I was upset, after visits from my parents, she was always ready with a cuddle and a chocolate biscuit to distract me.

"None of this is your fault," she told me. "You must remember that."

Thanks to Marie, and the kindness of the staff at the children's home, I was beginning to feel quite content. But one evening, towards the end of 1984, everything changed. As usual, me and the other kids were kicking up a fuss at bedtime; bouncing on the beds, shrieking and giggling as we ran between each other's rooms. The usual drill was for one of the staff to come in once, maybe twice, and threaten us with a punishment, before we eventually calmed down. The favoured punishment was a week's worth of early bedtimes, which nobody wanted. But on this particular night, for some reason, I was fizzed up, like a foamy glass of lemonade, spilling over the sides of the glass. Col, the most senior staff member, came to tell us all off once, and then again. The third time, when we heard his steps on the landing, my two roommates threw themselves under the duvet and into bed. But I was just too full of giggles and bubbles.

"I'm not gonna go to bed!" I announced, twirling round in my nightie; it had yellow flowers on which I loved.

Col stood in the doorway, his eyes blazing. I'd never seen him so annoyed. Before I had finished my twirl, he grabbed me by the ponytail and yanked me out of the room. The pain radiated across my scalp and in my terror, I felt a familiar, uncontrollable, rush down my legs.

"You dirty little cow, you've wet yourself," he hissed, through gritted teeth.

He opened another door, along the landing, and threw me on top of a bed. Then, he flicked the light off and slammed the door shut. I lay, sobbing and alone in the darkness, furious with myself for angering Col, mortified too that I had wet myself. What would everyone think of me now? I had really blown it this time. I had everything I needed here in this lovely home. And now, they were sure to throw me out. I'd have to start all over again. My mother was right, I thought bitterly. I was a waste of time and space. I was destined to end up just like her, with punters visiting me every day. The idea petrified me. And it was all because I'd misbehaved at bedtime. All night, I lay on top of the duvet with my wet nightie sticking to my legs. I grew trembly and cold, but still, I never budged. I deserved to shiver. I had ruined everything. And it was all my own fault. The next morning, I opened my door sheepishly, expecting the other girls to make fun of me. But it seemed Col had shocked them into silence too. I scrunched up my damp nightie and stuffed it behind my bedside table and then I got dressed ready for breakfast. Downstairs, I ran over to Col, desperate to make amends.

"I'm sorry," I said. "I'm really sorry for being naughty at bedtime. I won't ever do it again."

But he didn't even look at me. This was worse than I had thought. After breakfast, I helped clear away the plates and dishes, thinking he'd be impressed.

"Shall I make you a cuppa?" I asked. "Slice of toast, Col?"

But again, he didn't respond. As we lined up, ready to leave for school, I tried to catch his eye. And as we walked outside, I reached out for his hand. But he kept his in his pocket. He behaved as if I wasn't there. This, for me, was further confirmation my behaviour was way out of line. All day, at school, I had a horrible emptiness inside.

You've really blown it now, Hope. You stupid little slag.

It didn't once occur to me that Col was in the wrong. I was the one being punished, after all, so logically, I was at fault. I knew Col had such a difficult job, keeping order in the children's home, and I had made his life even worse. Day after day, I worried I'd gone too far, I was convinced I was about to be thrown out onto the street, away from everyone I'd grown to love. It was only as the days passed and conversation in the children's home turned to Christmas, that I finally began to relax a little. There was an annual Christmas party with a disco and a buffet. We all danced and played party games, and everyone got a small gift from a visiting Santa. After the remains of the egg sandwiches and the trifle were cleared away, we pulled back the rug in the main dining room and the music began. We danced all night to Wham! and Madonna, and even the staff let their hair down and joined in with the moves to *YMCA*. I felt a rush of joy as we all waved our hands above our heads. I belonged here. And it felt good.

"Last song!" shouted the DJ, who was one of our youth workers. "Everyone on the dance floor please."

It was the year of Band Aid and when *Do They Know It's Christmas?* blared from the speakers, I was suddenly overcome with a need to make peace. I ran to Col, who was sitting at a table by the door, drinking from a plastic cup, and I said: "Merry Christmas, Col. Thank you, thanks for everything you do for me. And I'm sorry, you know. I really am."

He pulled me towards him, so I was trapped between his legs, and planted a kiss right on my lips. Shocked, I pulled back, stumbling a little, and ran from the room. Upstairs, in my bedroom, I buried my head under my pillow and wept. I didn't really understand why I was crying; Col had forgiven me. Yet deep down, I knew it wasn't right. The sensation of his wet lips, slightly parted, on my mouth, still remained and I rubbed and rubbed at my face with the edge of the pillowcase. I thought back to the men who called on my mum. I remembered only too vividly the way they kissed her. 'Punter, or not?' Col was a punter; I was sure of it. I had spotted him. Just as he had spotted for me, for who I truly was.

You are a little slag. You are a little whore. You are a little slut.

7

THE NEW Year of 1985 brought with it more unwelcome shocks. One morning, I came down to breakfast, to be confronted by strange faces buttering toast and washing dishes.

"Where has everyone gone?" I demanded.

"New staff, new era," replied the woman in charge of the toast. "They've all moved on."

And just like that, without so much as a goodbye, my world was flipped upside down once again. Not just Col, but several of his colleagues too, had vanished, and I would never know why. Was it my fault? Was I to blame? My own mother didn't want me, so it made sense if they didn't want me either.

"Is it because I was naughty?" I asked, with a sickening realisation.

"Is it because I am infected?" I asked myself silently.

The new residential worker gave me no other reply than a hard stare as she set a plate full of toast down on the table. I shifted from one foot to the other, wanting a slice of toast but not feeling I could just help myself; not anymore. Over the next few weeks, I struggled to adjust to the new regime at the children's home. I didn't like the new staff, didn't want to like them, and I made my feelings clear. I was awkward and moody. And at the same time, I was on the edge of puberty and at a loss to deal with the confusing cascade of hormones. I had nobody to confide in. And so instead, I turned my pain inwards.

There was a group of girls, mainly older, who, in the evenings, would lock themselves in the biggest bathroom, for maybe an hour at a time. It was accepted, by the staff, that the girls liked to spend time in there, bathing, swapping make-up and doing each other's hair.

"Why can't I come in the bathroom?" I asked one of the older girls.

I was miserable. I felt excluded from everything. But she smiled at me and replied:

"You can! Ever had a chicken scratch? Come down later, after dinner, I'll show you how it's done."

I was intrigued. When the bathroom door locked behind us there was a ripple through the girls which was about more than excitement. It was intense; wired, febrile and ferocious. Jaya, one of the older girls, produced a handful of pennies from her pocket and handed them out.

"See," she showed me, rubbing the penny hard on her hand. "This is how you get a chicken scratch. Rub as hard as you can. Until you see blood."

I was so thrilled to be included, I began rubbing with enthusiasm. The girls around me were all doing the same thing. Only when our hands were red raw, with raised and bloody weals across our palms, did we pause. The release was wonderful. I leaned my head back, against the cool of the bathroom tiles, and I felt euphoric. The other girls all did the same. It was a collective sigh of relief. Reading fairytales was an escape, certainly. But this was on another level.

"Can I come tomorrow?" I asked eagerly, as I handed back my penny.

"Course," smiled Jaya.

It only took a few days for the staff to notice my hands.

"It's ridiculous behaviour," they told me angrily. "Stop it, or you'll lose your pocket money."

But I could not stop. I needed that one brief moment of respite. I craved that sense of togetherness with the other girls. To hide my scars from the staff, I began scratching my wrists instead. When that was spotted, I turned to scratching my thighs. Slowly, we moved on from pennies to razor blades and compasses. We even filed down pens and pencils to make them sharp. In the evenings, when we raided the kitchen, I always made a beeline for the locked cupboards which held the chocolate and sweets. But some girls tried to break the locks on the cutlery drawers, to get to the knives. We pounced on any sharp object we could find and hid it, until it was time to go to the bathroom. Part of the relief was certainly from the self-harming itself. But a huge draw, for us all, was that we did it together. There was a feeling of shared trauma and of understanding. Running compasses through our skin was a way of bonding and of acknowledging our own pain, and each other's. It didn't cure our agonies. But it helped, in some small way, to know we were all in it together.

Some of the girls, predictably, went too far. One evening, in the bathroom, I turned to see a girl leaning unsteadily over a sink filled with blood. In panic, we did our best to patch her up, but the bleeding was too heavy. She was rushed to hospital, and we never saw her again. Another girl had a fixation on pushing objects into her arm, small stationery items like erasers or pen tops. She too needed medical attention and she vanished also. I was careful, then, never to go too far. As much as I now hated my life at the children's home – and I did – I knew it could and would be much worse if I was moved elsewhere. We'd all heard appalling tales of sexual abuse and violence in other children's homes and secure units. We'd listened, with mounting dread, to lurid stories of Jimmy Savile, the bloke off the telly, given free access to the girls at one children's home. We knew of a rapacious paedophile who masqueraded as a caring staff member in another home.

The care circuit was a closed one; girls popped up again and again, our lives were overlapping and interwoven, for short periods at least. Everyone had a horror story to tell. And so I learned to be grateful that I was, at least, away from all that. I learned to be thankful that I was, at least, not being sexually abused. That was my level of expectation. Better the devil you know, I told myself. So to us, self-harming was just a part of our day. We scheduled it, after dinner and before bed, as though it was another activity.

Our perception of the world, and of ourselves, was so pitifully skewed, we did not see the damage we were doing. I thought self-harming happened in every children's home and maybe it did. I didn't, in essence, really see the harm in self-harming. I loved the way the atmosphere in the bathroom would change, as the cutting began. Beforehand, it was desperate, rushed, feverish. It was as though we had been inflated far too much, and we were about to pop. Afterwards, it was like someone had gone around with a valve and let a little bit of air out of each of us. It was so much more comfortable. For me, self-harming was like that first sip of wine on a Friday night after work, or a drag of a cigarette after a stressful day. It was liquid balm, running, soothingly, through my veins.

Aged 11, I was flabbergasted that the staff allowed us to huddle up together in a locked bathroom, night after night. I thought they were lenient and so gullible. Looking back now, I think they probably turned a blind eye. They were likely overwhelmed by the prospect of a dozen girls hacking away at their own bodies and they did not know what to do. Years later, in my medical notes, I learned I was on a waiting list for therapy to stop me self-harming. But I don't remember that.

Occasionally now, I meet professionals, or parents, who try to tell me self-harming is attention seeking. I could not disagree more strongly. I never self-harmed for attention. I did it because I was desperate. Because I was lost. Because I was broken. I didn't even want attention. Most of the time, I went to bed, wishing I wouldn't wake up. I used to envisage a button, which, if pressed, would kill me. I longed to press it. I longed to be free.

* * * *

Alongside self-harming, I began drinking more and sniffing aerosols. The relief which came from all three was as temporary as it was glorious, and the only way to replicate it was to do it again. I started absconding, at first just for an afternoon in the park, with a can of gas. Then, I'd stay out overnight, maybe even two nights. I missed day after day of school, and even when I was in class, I got into arguments and fights. I'd set the fire alarm off for a joke, so we'd all have to be evacuated, and then I'd run and run, as far away as I could get. I spent my afternoons hanging around with drunks on the streets or in squats. For me, this was not especially shocking, and it was not a new chapter, it was simply a return to the norm; a backwards slide into a world I knew only too well. If anything, I was climbing back onto the rails, not going off them. This was how I had been brought up, and this was how my parents lived their lives. This was the example I had been set. My only constant was Marie, my teacher.

"How's my little Hope today?" she would ask, as I marched into school, my face creased in frown. And that was enough, more than enough, to turn my whole day around. I loved being 'her Hope'. I cherished that feeling of belonging. Even now, the memory of it plucks at my heartstrings. As life became more tumultuous at the children's home, Marie took me under her wing more and more.

"How would you like to come to my house for tea one day?" she asked me.

My eyes grew round with astonishment.

"Really?" I shrieked. "Really?"

I threw my arms around her and, though I'd never felt happier, my eyes welled with tears. I was so grateful that someone actually wanted to spend time with me. That Friday, instead of going home with the other kids, I went home with Marie. I felt like the cat with the cream as I followed her across the teachers' car park. Her home was not the princess's castle of my imagination, but it was every bit as lovely. Three storeys, it had a basement kitchen where Marie made me crumpets and oatcakes. Her hallway was lined with family photographs, each one chronicling yet another happy occasion in their lives.

Marie's children arrived home soon after, one boy, one girl, along with their dad. I didn't like men at all, as a rule, but even I had to admit he was friendly and kind. Slightly bashful, I watched as the children played a game of roly-polies in the living room, and Marie joined in, standing with her legs wide so they could roll through. It was just a regular family scene, nothing special, yet this dynamic was completely alien to me. Alien – yet impossibly perfect. I had such a swell of longing in my chest that for a moment, the pain was unbearable. It felt like my breastbone would crack with the pressure. I wanted so much to be part of this, cocooned in love and stability. I laughed along with the others, but deep inside, I felt an ugly stab of jealousy, followed by a wave of shame. How come I didn't have a family? What was wrong with me? As if sensing my disquiet, Marie came and slipped her arm around me.

"You're doing really well, Hope," she said softly. "I am proud of you. Don't forget that. You'll always be my Hope."

Going back to the children's home, after a visit to Marie's, was hard. I even questioned whether it was worth experiencing such tenderness and happiness within the bosom of a family, because the crushing low which followed was almost unbearable. Lying on my bed, I felt angry, lonely and confused. Simon Le Bon stared impassively at me from my bedside poster, and I glared back.

"You can shut up," I snapped. "I never wanted to marry you anyway."

Towards the end of 1986, after yet another exclusion from school, yet another spell in a squat overnight, yet another showdown with the children's home staff, my social worker, Martha, took me out for a burger. As I chewed my first bite, she announced I was being moved to a secure unit. Away from my brothers, my friends, my bedroom. Away from everything I knew. Again.

"I don't want to go," I protested, my voice rising. "I'm not going. I refuse."

Right there, in the café, I was so furious, so cut adrift, that I could not even cry. The burger sat in my mouth. As it congealed, the anger built and built inside me, like a dam about to burst.

"I'm not going," I said again.

But as usual, it wasn't up to me. My stuff was packed and already in the social worker's car. It felt like such a cruel trick, using a lousy burger to blackmail me out of the children's home, and my stomach roiled in protest. I wasn't even allowed back to the home to say my goodbyes.

"Look Hope, it's the best thing for you," my social worker said. "You will have lessons in the unit, so you'll get a proper education. You can't keep running away."

"You see if I can't," I mumbled, as I climbed into the back seat and slammed the door shut.

We'd all heard the stories about the secure units, how they were crammed with hardened criminals, housed behind locked doors. I might as well have been packed off to Pentonville prison. I felt rejected, conned and lied to. I felt absolutely rudderless, as though I was a scrap of litter, caught in the London breeze. I had no control over my future, no idea where I would land next. I was angry too; livid even. But drowning out all the other emotions was a sense of self-loathing. As usual, I blamed myself. I had brought this on myself.

You are a little slut. You are a little slag. You are a little whore.

8

THE SECURE unit was a huge modern building, in another area of London. From the outside, it was faceless, uninviting and unfriendly. There was a row of square windows, with a light in each. One for every cell. Inside, it was painted off-white and there was a strong smell of disinfectant, with a whiff of urine and cigarette smoke stirred in. We went through so many locked doors, I began to think I really was going to prison, after all. The social worker pointed out the classrooms, the bathrooms, the bedrooms, along the way.

"There is everything you need in here, so no reason to leave," she said, as though that was somehow a good thing.

My skin prickled with fear, and I felt my throat tightening. What if I never left? What if I was locked in here forever, stifled, choked, suffocated? Who would miss me? Who would care? A tidal wave of terror sloshed over me, I felt my arms and legs flailing, I heard a voice screaming. I realised it was me.

"In you go," said a stranger's voice, and I was lifted off my feet as he launched me into a room. The floor, like the walls, was padded. There was a beanbag, but nothing else. Not even a window.

"This is wrong!" I screamed. "I shouldn't be in prison! I'm only 13!"

A hatch in the door was snapped open like the jaws of a crocodile.

"Calm down, and then you can come out," said the same voice.

I didn't want to be in there, but neither did I want to come out. I was petrified of what I might find. But eventually, I exhausted myself, through crying and wailing. As I sank back onto the beanbag, with my head in my hands, the door was unlocked and opened.

"Come with me," said one of the youth workers.

Warily, I followed him into a living room which had an office off to one side, with glass windows. There was a group of other girls, all at least a couple of years older than me, pushing each other around and exchanging abuse. The staff, in the office, sat and watched.

"She's new," said one, cocking her head towards me. "You fancy a go, fatty?"

She cackled and I shrank back in alarm, bracing myself. I couldn't work out why the staff weren't intervening. Luckily for me, she spotted a second contender, who ran in, fists flying.

"Come on!" yelled the first girl.

It was as though she'd thrown a grenade. The entire room exploded. There were girls standing on the table, others throwing chairs. There was punching, scratching and stamping. The office door was briskly locked, and the staff scurried like mice, behind a desk. I was swept along on a wave of nauseous exhilaration, dodging the flying furniture and the punches. The fight spilled over into the corridors and, as the living room quietened a little, I felt my arm twisted sharply up my back, as I was shoved to the floor. There was a knee in the small of my back, crushing my kidneys, squashing the breath out of me. I couldn't even scream. With my face pressed into the dusty carpet, I began choking. It took a few moments for me to come to my senses and then I tried fighting back, wriggling and kicking up my legs. I couldn't work out why the staff weren't coming to help me.

"Keep still," hissed a man's voice. The same voice which had earlier told me to calm down in the padded cell.

And then, it hit me. The staff weren't helping because the staff were the ones attacking me. I was dragged back to the padded cell and locked up again. All evening, way after the pain had subsided, my shoulder ached and ached.

"You've done something to my shoulder," I said, when I was finally let out. "I need a doctor."

But he wasn't interested. Fast-forward nearly four decades, and I still have nagging aches in my back and shoulders. I've recently been diagnosed with fibromyalgia and in my mind, the damage was done that first day, on the unit.

The following day, the anarchy continued. The living room was more like a bear pit, with older girls – and even staff – baiting the others to fight. And after instigating a riot, the staff just locked themselves in the office and chaos reigned. The girls didn't fight over serious disagreements or grievances. Mostly, they simply wanted something to do, something to remind themselves they were still alive. In the afternoon, I found the fire alarm and I smashed it. During the evacuation, I ran away. And after they brought me back, I smashed it again. It became a daily pattern. I didn't get further than a few streets away, but it felt good to rebel. I was doing something at least to let them know how utterly miserable I was. But as usual, my tactics backfired. Each time I was brought back, I was strip searched. And then I ended up in the padded cell, with only a plastic beanbag for company.

"I'm not staying here," I vowed. "I'm a child. This isn't fair."

Fighting the system, I knew, was possibly the worst thing I could do. Yet I had no other options. And besides, I didn't care. I couldn't have felt any more hopeless, no matter what punishments they gave me. The first chance I got, I smashed the fire alarm, and I was out of there again. Several of us scarpered, laughing manically as we raced down the street, arms waving, whooping as though we'd made it out of Alcatraz. The chasing youth workers couldn't keep up. The best thing about freedom was the smell. After the bleachy, pissy, miserable stench of the unit, the smell of fresh air in my nostrils was divine. I gulped in deep lungfuls, unaware how polluted it really was, and it would not have mattered to me anyway. First of all, I ran back to the children's home, and my brothers greeted me with delight. But as the soon as a staff member spotted me, my house of cards came tumbling down yet again.

"Hope, you can't stay here," she said sadly. "I'm sorry."

She was already dialling the secure unit, and I turned and ran. Two days later, the police found me in a squat, partially dressed, soaked in sweat and urine, drugged, drunk and terrified. I had little or no recollection of where I'd been or what I'd been doing. When I arrived back at the unit, instead of letting me shower and change, a staff member frogmarched me into the living room.

"She's back, Miss Pissy-pants," he announced. "Look at the

state of her. She's filthy. She stinks. That's what happens when you run away."

The other girls were invited to pass comment on my clothes, as though I was some sort of freak show, paraded in the room purely for their entertainment.

"Smelly cow!"

"Jesus Christ, look at her jeans."

"What's that stain? Has she shit herself? Keep her away from me."

After I'd showered, I found my dirty clothes at the bottom of the bed.

"You'll wash those yourself," I was told. "Learn your lesson."

I felt absolutely wretched. I was enveloped by loneliness, and the anger burned still. I felt let down and abandoned, by Marie, by the children's home, by my parents. But mostly, by myself.

Later that same day, I smashed the fire alarm and ran away again. The staff knew what I was up to, yet they had no choice but to follow rules when the fire alarm was activated. It gave me time to run up the road as fast as I could and disappear into the anonymising streets of London. I came across a park bench, and I pulled my gas cannister out of my pocket. It wasn't long before a middle-aged man came to sit next to me. Of course a young girl sniffing gas during the day is a magnet for paedophiles. I thought I knew everything there was to know, but I was incredibly naïve.

"You wanna watch a porno?" he asked me, with a salacious smile.

I snorted in disgust.

"No!" I replied.

"Well, why not come back to my flat?" he suggested. "We

won't watch a film. We can just have a drink. I've got a few cans. You'll get picked up by the police, sitting here when you should be at school."

He was right about that, I conceded. And as long as we didn't watch a dirty film, I saw no harm in going back to his flat. I was cold, anyway, on the bench, and it was boring too.

"Ok," I agreed.

I followed him to a high-rise block and up to his flat. It was filthy and smelled of dogs and dirty old men. It seemed so much worse too, in comparison with the sterility of the secure unit. Perching on the end of a sticky sofa, I felt horribly uncomfortable. He handed me a can of lager, and sat down next to me, whilst he fiddled with the TV remote.

My heart quickened a little as the porno he had promised not to show me began to play. I felt his hand force its way down under my jogging bottoms. It wasn't difficult to bypass the elasticated waistband and I cursed myself for not wearing jeans or fitted trousers, something, anything, to keep his greasy fingers out. I wore jogging bottoms because I was overweight, because I was embarrassed at my figure. So this was my fault. I was to blame that he was touching me. I'd messed up, yet again.

The fingers found their way into my underwear, and I felt a sudden shooting pain. Squeezing my eyes closed, I pictured myself retreating, through the back of the sofa, and into my very own fairytale. In my story, I was a little red and black ladybug, curled up into the tiniest ball, to keep the predators away. I concentrated very hard on being the best ladybug I could. When it was over, and he stood up, I dared to open my eyes again. I was a little taken aback not to have a red shell and two tentacles. I didn't speak, I didn't move. I stayed curled in my little ball, until eventually I heard a police officer talking to me.

"What's your name? Can you tell me where you live?"

I mumbled the name of the secure unit and he and his colleague exchanged weary glances.

"Another one. Waste of our time, these kids."

I was driven back to the unit, and nobody asked me about the man or what had taken place inside his flat. The staff were annoyed with me for running away and causing a fuss. I was ordered to shower, and when I came back, into the living room, my dirty clothes were in a pile on the floor.

"Look at Pissy-Pants' filthy clothes," jeered one of the youth workers, holding up my knickers by the tips of his fingers, as if they were crawling with maggots. "See how dirty she is."

In bed that night, I curled up again, as tightly as I could, with my knees right under my chin. If I was a cute little ladybug, I'd be able to just fly away from this. Instead, I was fat, dirty and ugly, and I was stuck here. I thought again of the end-of-life button; one press, dead in an instant. My fingertips itched to press it.

9

DESPITE MY fantasies about the suicide button, there was a stubbornness deep inside me, like a small nut hidden inside a shell, which just would not give way and would not give up. And despite the punishments, despite the taunts and the cruelty, I never lost my fighting spirit. Most days, it did me no favours. I answered back when I was told off. I ran away every single chance I got. When I was physically restrained, I fought back. To the staff, I am sure, it looked as though I was on a path of self-destruction. But it was my way of staying strong, my approach to staying alive. No matter what was said, or what they did, a small spark glowed within me, and it kept me warm.

Worse though, than being punished myself, was seeing others punished. I could not bear to see the other kids, especially the more vulnerable ones, being bullied or hurt. Still, from caring for my baby brothers, I had a residual maternal streak and a sense of responsibility. Each time I tried to step in to protect a girl from the staff, I was just wrestled to the ground myself. It was pointless. And yet, I couldn't stand by and do nothing. I felt like such a coward. Such a wimp. The staff seemed to pick up on this, because they'd bring me into the living room when someone else was being disciplined, so I was forced to watch. I felt the child's pain as acutely as if it was my own and, though I closed my eyes, and tried to distract myself, I felt that familiar rush between my legs. My shoulders sagged as the youth worker swivelled to face me.

"You dirty cow!" he yelled. "Pissy-pants is at it again. Look everyone! You can wash those knickers yourself."

As I trailed wearily down to the bathroom to scrub my underwear, he made sure everyone knew about my accident. And no matter how many times I rinsed them, I wasn't sure I'd ever get rid of the smell. Lying in bed that night, I reminded myself that I had willingly walked into the police station and surrendered myself, and my brothers, into the care of the system. I had marched into this trap with my eyes wide open. I was responsible for my suffering. It was all my own fault.

That same night, dreaming of Dad and his large black coat, dreaming of the kittens I found in the bin, I longed for home. I even missed my mother, her bright red lips, her high heels, her drunken rantings. I missed everything I knew. Yet in truth, it was not so much my home that I longed for, as the concept of home. And it was much easier to be nostalgic when I was no longer there. The next morning, I'd wet the bed. I did my best to dry it with a towel and hide the patch under the duvet. But as always, it was the penetrating smell that gave me away.

"Pissy-pants!" shouted one of the staff, as I ate my breakfast. "You need to come and wash your bedding. Now."

Washing my own sheets by hand was impossible. I couldn't get the suds out. I couldn't squeeze out the excess water. The tears fell into the soapy water, and again, I missed my home. My brothers. My school. My old self.

"Pissy-pants!" rapped a youth worker, as he walked past the bathroom. "Get a move on!"

I had made myself a target for the staff. I knew that. I had pitted myself against them and I was determined not to be beaten. I ran away at every opportunity and when I was brought back, I refused to leave my room. I didn't even go out for mealtimes.

"Not hungry," I snarled, when they opened the door hatch. "Leave me alone."

One night, I heard a commotion, lots of giggling and shouting, and I realised some of the older girls had been allowed out for the evening.

"Get pissy-pants!" someone shouted. "She'll eat it. She eats anything. Look how fat she is."

Minutes later, the hatch opened, and I was told:

"Get dressed. You're getting up."

There was no point in me resisting. They'd just drag me out otherwise. In the living room, one of the staff nodded at a bin. I peered inside and saw a half-eaten kebab.

"There's your dinner," he smirked. "We know how much you like your food."

I looked from one face to the next, desperately hoping this was a joke. But each one stared back in expectation, waiting for the show to begin. I might as well have been a dancing bear with a chain around my leg.

"Eat it, eat it, eat it," chanted the girls.

As I lifted it out of the bin, I almost retched. There were bite marks in the bread, and the sauce had spread all down the side of the bin. There was rubbish in there too, bits of paper sticking to the sauce. I couldn't believe they were going to make me eat this. It was beyond cruel. But the staff were chanting just as enthusiastically as the girls. I had nobody on my side.

"Go on then," said one of the staff, more sharply now. "Pick the kebab up and eat it."

I had no choice but to do as they said. I chewed each mouthful, trying to ignore the bits of rubbish and wrapping that I was eating. I was being watched with interest as though I was some sort of specimen, wheeled out of my room to be experimented upon.

How much can she take?

And that was where, despite the barbarity, I had the upper hand. Because I could take whatever they doled out. And more. As a little girl, I'd hardened and calcified, because I had to. That little nut, nestling under layers and layers of shell, was shiny and intact. These people would not break me, I was sure of that. I finished the kebab and wiped my mouth with the back of my sleeve. Grotesquely, I walked out of the room to rapturous applause, as though I'd just delivered a top-class performance. On my way down the hallway, I smashed the fire alarm, and then I ran. And this time, I had no intention of going back.

* * * *

"No way I'm going back there, it's like a zoo," I told my social worker, when I was eventually picked up by the police.

And so, after less than a month in the unit, I was moved again. A room in a second secure unit was found for me, and I reasoned it couldn't be any worse than the first one. I was wrong. Superficially, the second place looked much the same as the first. There was the same standard issue hospital furniture, a wooden bed, nailed to the floor, with a plastic blue mattress on the top. There was a hatch in the door so that I could be monitored, hourly. It made me feel like a high-profile serial killer, the way the beam shone through my door at 3am, 4am, 5am, all through those lonely hours. I never got used to it. My sleep was broken and splintered. I was only just dozing off from one check, when it was time for the next one.

"Why do you have to keep waking me up, every hour?" I complained.

"Check you're breathing," was the monotone reply before the hatch snapped shut again.

"I am, unfortunately," I retorted.

I wished sometimes the torch could shine a light right through me and into my soul. If they could see how sad I was, how much I was suffering, surely, they would let me out of here. My spirit was withering in this unit. It was so hard to stay upright, to stay proud. At a meeting with my social worker, later that week, I agreed to try to change my behaviour.

"You've gotta stop running away, Hope," she told me. "If you keep absconding, you are giving the court a reason to keep you in this place. If you show you can be trusted, they will let you out soon."

It felt counter-intuitive to pretend I loved the place, but I could see her logic and I decided to take her advice. Though I was mistrustful of the other girls, I hated the loneliness of my room too, and so I spent as much time as I could in the living room, which was the only communal area. There was a big sofa in there and we were allowed to play music when our lessons were done. In the corner, was a dining table and chairs. The food came up in a lift from the kitchen on the ground floor. The furniture was all standard issue, the type you'd find in a hospital – fire resistant, wipe down, cheap plastic. The living room sofa was made of blue plastic, not dissimilar to the mattresses. Everything was bolted to the floor. The choice of furniture was a reflection of how much the staff didn't trust us. They expected trouble, and we didn't disappoint. Yet despite the fights and the punishments, those times in the living room were probably the most bearable. I heard UB40 for the first time and I loved them. The lyrics seemed to speak directly to me.

Nobody knows me
Even though I'm always there
A statistic, a reminder
Of a world that doesn't care.

One evening, we were lying back on the sofa, higgledy-piggledy, arms and legs flung out, listening to UB40. One of the youth workers, Jonno, walked in and I groaned inwardly when he plonked himself down, right in the middle of us all. Jonno was tall and stick thin, with distant, pale blue eyes and purple threads which ran across his cheeks, like maps in blood.

"Alright girls?" he grinned, and it sounded flirtatious, indecent.

He slung his arm across the back of the couch, and then let it drop casually around my shoulder. His fingers inched across my T-shirt until they reached the edge of my bra. I sucked my breath in, petrified to move, even to breathe. If I stirred at all, he could be in there, inside my T-shirt. I stole a sideways glance at his face, but he was looking straight ahead, his jawline jutting out in smug arrogance. The girls around me didn't really seem to have noticed. Or if they had, it didn't register with them.

Jonno's finger ends scorched through my T-shirt. The material seemed to dissolve like acid. His hands were on my bare skin. I felt so exposed. And then, I found myself on my feet. Without knowing it would happen, I'd jumped up off the sofa, and I was running across the room, away from Jonno. My legs had taken a decision when my brain would not.

"What's wrong with you?" he asked, in mock surprise.

I said nothing. But I picked a chair at the far side and sat down, determined not to show I was rattled. Minutes later, I saw Jonno's hand snaking across another girl's T-shirt. She sat stock-still, petrified, as his fingers slowly made their way under her clothing. I wanted to scream out. Why had nobody noticed? Why was nobody objecting? I watched, transfixed, as Jonno patted her knee and silently, they both stood up and left the room.

"We all know where they're going," smirked one of the girls. "Jonno is a dirty bastard. He really is."

I was sickened. It was appalling that the other girls were so conditioned to accept such perverted behaviour, they barely thought it worth a mention. But I felt lucky too, that I at least recognised it was wrong.

"Why don't the staff do something?" I asked limply, knowing full well how stupid that sounded.

The other girls laughed heartily in reply as if they'd never heard anything so silly. From then, I kept an eye on Jonno and as the weeks passed, I realised he was a serial offender. He picked on the quiet girls, the ones who didn't kick up a fuss. It was yet more confirmation, for me, that I was right to fight back. I was right to make a nuisance of myself. I was a handful, and I was a mouthpiece. And so, he left me alone. More trouble than she's worth, that one. But it was torture, watching the other girls follow him out of the living area, like little lambs off to the abattoir.

He was easily twice, maybe three times their age. He was an adult. They were children. He was a residential youth worker. They were vulnerable and in his care. The injustice screamed at me, and I was desperate to help but knew at the same time, I could not. Some of the girls saw nothing wrong with what he did. Others begged me not to make a fuss, because it would land them in trouble. It was pointless confiding about this – or any aspect of the abuse – in my social worker. I had seen, from bitter experience, that girls who reported back to their social worker were then returned to the unit and punished harder than ever before. It seemed there was no way out of it. I was grateful to be spared Jonno's bony, wandering fingers. But the little devil on my shoulder, the cruel voice in my head, told me that he fancied all the other girls – except me.

"Why not you, Hope?" asked the voice. "Why doesn't he choose you?"

I knew the answer. He didn't choose me because I was dirty and dislikeable. I was infected and unabusable. I was a little whore. I was a little slag. I was a little slut.

10

AS THE weeks became months in the secure unit, my spirit was pared down, bent over and damaged, like a flower in the wind. Yet it never broke completely. I realised the sense in my social worker's advice too. It was useless to keep fighting back. Pointless to keep running away. Slowly, reluctantly, I became more compliant. I hoped, by stealth, I could beat these people at their own game. And so it was. Because six months on, the court order to keep me in a secure unit expired.

Now that I had stopped absconding and raising hell every day, there were no grounds to apply for an extension of the order. Instead, I was told I would be moving to a new children's home. It was a long way out of London. Far from everyone I knew. I could not decide whether that was a good or a bad thing. I was moving far from my family and friends, far from the teachers and social workers I'd grown close to. The court finally took account of my request for all contact with my parents to be stopped completely too.

There were to be no letters, no phone calls, no visits. They were not even permitted to know where I lived. To me, as a mother now, it's utterly tragic for a child to have to ask a court to keep her parents away. It's bizarre too. But as a 13-year-old,

I was used to it. I was accustomed to my parents throwing hand grenades into my life and then standing back to watch me burn. And I needed it to stop.

"It's a fresh start for you, Hope," said my social worker. "I hope you'll make the most of it."

I had no idea what lay ahead. But I felt pretty sure it had to be better than the place I was leaving behind. My new home, an old mansion house, was at the end of a long drive and set in extensive grounds. Even before I'd stepped inside, I was falling in love with the place, swooning at the ornate window frames, the imposing front door, the manicured lawns. This house was straight out of a fairytale.

"We're really happy to have you here," smiled Tom, one of the staff, who showed me around. The house was divided into separate units, each unit having a few single bedrooms, a small kitchen and a bathroom. We were encouraged to look after ourselves, to prepare snacks, make toast or a boiled egg maybe, but the main meals were prepared by a team of cooks and served in a huge dining room. I whooped in excitement when I saw my bedroom door had no hatch. There were no locks on the doors. No bolts holding the furniture down.

"This place is like a palace," I smiled.

In a large, communal area there was a pool table and a pin-ball machine. It just got better and better. That first night, I had the best sleep, with no torch poking through the door every hour to check I was alive. The next morning, I went down for breakfast. I knew some of the girls already; we'd followed similar paths through the care system, and they were mostly friendly. But that first morning, as I queued for my cereal, I felt a sharp prod in my back and a voice said:

"Alright fatty? You gonna eat the lot or you gonna save some for me?"

Her words scalded. Suddenly I was painfully aware of the way my T-shirt strained a little across my belly. I was fat, she was right. And now everyone else knew it too.

"Oi, fatty, I'm talking to you," she said again.

I didn't dare turn around. I didn't want to get into trouble, not so soon. The trauma of the secure unit was fresh in my mind, and there was no way I was going back there. I looked straight ahead and tried to ignore her, hoping she might find someone else to pick on.

"That's Tiffany," one of the other girls, Lara, whispered, as we poured our milk. "Take no notice, she's a bully. She's the same with me."

I ate my cereal and didn't let it bother me. I'd come across much worse than her, after all. She kept up the same routine for most of that week. She even had a little entourage around her, chirping like obedient budgies, every time she slung an insult my way.

"You fat cow, you don't need breakfast. You look like you've had enough."

On the fourth morning, when I got out of bed, I made my decision. And as I waited for breakfast, I was aware of Tiffany shoving her way through the line, to get to me. As her short finger prodded me between the shoulder blades, I spun around, before she even had a chance to speak. I drew back my arm and smacked her full in the face, knocking her backwards. She landed in an ungainly mess in the middle of her little gang.

"Leave me alone," I hissed.

It was the only way I knew. It was also the best and most effective way to deal with a bully.

"I enjoyed that," Lara told me, with a smile. "I've been trying to pluck up the courage to stand up to her for months."

"She won't bother you again now," I said to Lara. "Don't worry about her."

Sure enough, Tiffany left us both well alone. There were times when I wanted to thank her; it was because of her bullying that Lara and I got to know each other. Over those first few weeks, we became inseparable. I'd never had a best friend and I'd always longed for a sister. Lara filled both of those roles.

She was incredibly pretty; slim and feminine, with gorgeous, long dark hair and wide eyes. We did our lessons together, inside the children's home, and we were encouraged to take up hobbies too. I was astonished. Nobody had ever thought I was worthy of a hobby before! I had always wanted to learn the drums, and Lara signed up for guitar lessons.

"Let's form a band," I said.

We started practising together, most evenings. We had polarising tastes; Lara was into hard rock, whilst I remained steadfastly faithful to Duran Duran. As a compromise, we learned to play Led Zeppelin's *Stairway to Heaven*. We planned a concert, for all the staff and children, and even some visitors too. Lara couldn't wait, she was a natural performer and a talented musician. I, on the other hand, had enthusiasm on my side, but not much else. As the day drew nearer, I started to worry.

"You'll be fine," Lara reassured me. "It will be a laugh."

But when I took my place on the makeshift stage, and looked out into the audience, my nerves began jangling. I could barely hold the drumsticks; I was shaking so badly. And in the first few bars of the song, I lost my timing. In dismay, I threw down my sticks and ran out of the room. Lara finished the performance on her own.

"Sorry," I said to her, later. "I feel such a fool."

She just laughed it off. Nothing much bothered Lara; it was one of the reasons we got on so well. My drum lessons continued, and I began working towards my Duke Of Edinburgh award too. I was the only girl in our group who wanted to study history, and it wasn't included on the limited curriculum inside the children's home. So instead, I was offered a private tutor.

"Yes please!" I smiled.

The opportunities felt endless. We were so well looked after and cared for and after the secure unit, it was a culture shock. One of the staff taught me how to flower-arrange and I enjoyed it so much, she offered to take me out to the churches she worked at, arranging displays before Sunday service. There was a sewing teacher too. I loved crafts of all kinds, and I really thrived in her classes.

Best of all were the evenings, snuggled on the sofa with the staff, watching films or playing board games. I loved cuddles; I'd grown up starved of affection and love. The kindness of the staff helped, in some way, to plug the gaping void left by the lack of a family, and the absence of parental care.

"I absolutely love it here," I told Lara, as we queued for supper.

One weekend, the staff announced we all had appointments at the hairdressers. I was beside myself with excitement. Lara and I both decided to go for a perm, in keeping with the fashion of the late '80s. I had a soft perm, and my hair was cut into a bob. Lara kept her long hair, and she chose a corkscrew perm. I loved my new hairstyle. I loved my new home. Best of all, I loved my new friend. Lara went home at weekends, to see her parents and her brother, and I was always lost without her.

"Won't be the same without you," I told her.

It was difficult, seeing most of the other girls go home on Friday evenings. I didn't want to see my own parents. Yet it saddened me to think of how life could and should have been. For most kids, being in care was difficult because they were separated from their parents. For me, being in care was a way of escaping from my parents.

11

I HAD been in the children's home for several weeks when it dawned on me I hadn't self-harmed once. I'd been so busy, making new friends, doing homework and music practice, flower-arranging and sewing, that I hadn't felt the urge. I hadn't even thought about it. After dinner, when our chores were done, the staff would usually put a film on in the living room and we'd all pile on the big sofas together. I didn't need to self-harm because there was nothing I wanted to run away from.

But one evening, an older girl ushered us all into the bathroom and locked the door, and I had a familiar feeling of expectancy. Instead of a compass, she produced a bottle of Indian ink and a needle.

"Who wants a tattoo?" she asked, with a gleam in her eye.

"Me!" I volunteered, rolling up my sleeve.

I didn't care that she wasn't trained. Or that she'd never even done a tattoo before. The health and hygiene aspect didn't occur to me, or to anyone else.

"What d'you want?" she asked, as though she had an extensive menu for me to choose from.

I settled on a rose, with a leaf at the side, and I held out my wrist. The process was far more painful than I'd anticipated, and the finished product looked like a large red splodge.

"Well, I need some practice," she grinned. "You're my first one."

I laughed. I didn't mind. I was just pleased to have a tattoo. I felt really grown up, part of the gang. I was finally starting to believe I belonged somewhere. And then, my teacher had an idea which just cemented that feeling even more. I'd shown a flair for creative subjects, such as sewing, flower-arranging and craft. And he suggested I might enjoy design and technology classes.

"Yes, I would," I told him. "I love anything practical. Anything at all."

"We don't offer these lessons here," he explained. "You'd need to join in lessons at a local school."

With my heart sinking, I listened, waiting for the 'but.' There was always a 'but' where I was concerned.

"So," he said. "What do you think? Do you fancy it?"

I was dumbfounded. I couldn't believe the staff would trust me to leave the premises and attend a real school, for a start. And the fact someone had gone to so much trouble, just for me, really touched my heart.

"I'd love it," I said eventually. "Thank you."

I was enrolled to study design and technology at a local school, twice a week. The staff at the children's home bought me a uniform, and I was almost more thrilled about that than I was about the lessons themselves. I wore a navy-blue skirt and jumper, and a pair of black Kickers. I looked at myself in the mirror, with my permed bob, my smart uniform, and for the first time ever, I liked what I saw. I loved having a uniform. I loved being just another kid, part of the pack. In the local high school, I had no labels, no behaviour plans, no special report. I was just Hope, studying design. If the other pupils were curious or wary of me, they didn't show it. I made friends with a boy called David in my class, who came to sit on my desk and chat at the end of each lesson.

"Oh Lara," I said dreamily when I got back to the children's home. "He's got gelled hair. Gorgeous eyes. I think I'm in love."

"Thought you loved Simon le Bon?" she said.

"I love them both," I conceded. "Equally."

I was too shy to tell David how I felt, and I had no idea whether he felt the same. But I needed to make my devotion official, somehow. So the next time the home-made tattoo kit made an appearance, I offered my arm.

"Can I have DP?" I asked. "David's initials? I want him with me forever."

Lara giggled.

"You sure you want a lifelong reminder of this boy?" she asked, as I rolled up my sleeve. "You've never even kissed him, Hope!"

But I had made up my mind. I was completely infatuated. The tattoo was a little blurry and little too blue, but it was free of charge and, I told myself proudly, it was an enduring symbol of my love. The next time I went into school, I so embarrassed that I pulled my jumper down over my wrist, and wrapped it round my fingers, to hide the tattoo. I realised I couldn't possibly show it to David. Not yet anyway. I tried to concentrate on my work, and David helped me with the finishing touches of a wooden dressing table I was building, as part of my coursework.

"It's really good, Hope," he said, ignoring the rickety legs and the obvious lean.

"Thanks," I smiled, still with my jumper pulled down over my wrist.

I passed my design and technology exam with flying colours. The instructor seemed quite impressed with my wobbly dressing table. As for David, I never saw him again after the course finished. To this day, I have DP on my arm, and yet I can't even remember what the P stands for! Lara was right all along.

As well as my friendships with the girls, I bonded especially well with two staff members, Callum and Issy. Callum was one of the residential social workers, Issy was a cleaner. Callum was strict but fair. Issy was kind and patient. She was pretty too, with lots of curls.

"Another Disney princess, just like Marie," I told myself.

Even as a teenager, I was still clinging to the fairytale. Issy was great fun too, she wore a Walkman whilst she was cleaning, so we'd sneak up behind her to make her jump. When she'd got her breath back, she let me listen to her Walkman and I was amazed to hear Guns n Roses playing. She was another unlikely hard rock fan, just like Lara.

"You look too sweet to be listening to that rubbish," I said. "What's wrong with Duran Duran?"

Issy groaned and rolled her eyes. Everyone knew about my obsession with Simon Le Bon.

"I wish you could have been my mum," I told Issy one day, as she took a break from hoovering. "I think you'd make a great mother."

Everyone knew also about my obsession with having my own foster family. I was desperate for a home of my own. With each year that passed, the hope faded a little more. But a small glimmer still remained. Issy smiled and tucked her curls away from her face.

"That's a nice thing to say," she replied. "Who would you choose as your dad?"

"Callum," I said immediately. "I really like Callum. In fact, you and he could be my foster mum and dad! Why don't you two get together?"

She laughed and gave me a gentle push.

"Oh Hope, you and your imagination. It runs away with you sometimes. You read too many stories."

But the idea unfurled, slowly, like a seedling inside my mind, and it grew and grew. The more I thought about it, the more I realised they were perfect for each other. I knew they were both single and so I set about playing matchmaker.

"Hey Callum, why don't you take Issy out tonight?" I asked. "You know how pretty she is. She told me she likes you too."

And when I saw Issy, I reminded her:

"I want you and Callum as my foster mum and dad, so you'd better get it together. Do it for my sake! You know how nice he is. He told me he really likes you. Honestly. He said he loves your curls."

It was only a white lie, I told myself. Everyone loved Issy's curls. Whether it was my scheming, or whether fate played a hand, I will never know. But a few weeks later, I spotted Callum and Issy walking into work hand in hand.

"Yes!" I whooped, racing down the hall to meet them. "You can be my real foster mum and dad now!"

Their romance flourished and became a long-term relationship. I was thrilled and I really felt they had me to thank for giving them the push they needed. When they moved in together, Issy announced I could be their first visitor.

"You serious?" I asked, my eyes alight with pride.

They were busy renovating their new home, and so I was allowed to write: 'Hope woz 'ere' on the wall, before it was decorated. It makes me smile to think my juvenile graffiti will still be there, even now. Issy made me cheese and biscuits and took me shopping. Everyone at the home had a TV in their bedroom, but I didn't. So on one visit, she took me out and bought me a portable telly. I was over the moon.

"I'll think of you every time I watch it," I promised.

On my next visit, she and Callum took me to a theme park. After an afternoon screaming on the roller-coasters, we went out for tea to the local pub.

"You know, you're the best foster mum and dad I could ever wish for," I told them.

"And you're the best matchmaker," Issy smiled. "You're our very own Cilla Black."

I beamed. I'm sure Callum and Issy would have got together without my persuasion. Even so, I like to think I had a hand in it. They were my proof you're never too old for a fairytale ending.

12

ONE OF the rewards for good behaviour at the children's home was book tokens, which we could earn by behaving well in class, or helping out with jobs around the place. Each good deed was recorded on a 'status chart' and it was my ambition to get to the very top of it. I washed the staff cars. I picked up litter in the grounds. I also earned tokens for working hard in history because this was an extra-curricular commitment.

For me, a book token was something to be treasured. My love of reading had started as a little girl, when I created alternate universes for myself, fairytale realities, away from the depravity and the suffering of my own childhood. As I grew older, my hobby became a passion. At each new unit, or children's home, I'd ask immediately if I could borrow a book. Novels were an escape, a time-out, a chance to snatch a little scrap of vicarious happiness.

It was bewildering to me that many of the girls at the children's home were not interested in reading. They were happy to pass their own book tokens on to me, which meant even more new books. In addition to tokens, good behaviour was rewarded with takeaways or film nights, or late bedtimes at weekends. There were so many incentives to be good. About once a month, the staff would take me into town, on a Saturday, to spend my tokens at WHSmith.

"If you carry on behaving so well, you'll have your own library soon," they told me.

Marie, my old teacher, had stayed in touch, weaving in and out of my life like a golden thread. She often brought me a book, or even posted one, with a little note attached.

'Thought you'd enjoy this one, Hope. Lots of lovely adjectives. Keep up the reading!'

I didn't need any encouragement. After fairytales and young children's books, I moved on to Roald Dahl. I let him carry me away inside his imagination, and it was a real adventure. As I hit my teens, I began reading *Sweet Valley High*, and devoured the whole series. I loved *The Secret Diary of Adrian Mole* too. During one trip into town, I bought a book called *Flowers In The Attic* by V.C. Andrews. The narrative, about children who are locked in an attic by their cruel mother, had so many similarities to my own life and I became preoccupied by it. I couldn't put it down. I identified with the teenage daughter in the book, who was left to look after her younger siblings, as I was. The narrative was twisted and deranged and deeply moving. There were many echoes of my own childhood, and I sobbed as I read it. I found it so hard to read, and yet I could not put it down.

My next review reported I was making good progress, and recommended I should be allowed to get a Saturday job, in a bakery in town. I was thrilled to have a job, just like the tattoo, and the design classes, I felt a part of something. I was a cog in a wheel, an ingredient in a recipe, and I loved it. And, as with the design classes, the uniform really outweighed the joy of the job itself. Looking back, it was the sort of uniform most teenagers would flatly refuse to wear in public. But I was really proud of it. I had a straw hat and a beige dress with a red tabard over the top. For me, it was a sign of success.

"You can go on the bus to work on your own," Callum told me. "We trust you."

That first trip was strangely daunting. I'd been outside on my own hundreds of times, without permission. At the secure units, I'd spent more nights on the streets than I had in my bed. Yet now, with nobody chasing me, with nobody to run from, I felt obscurely anxious, as though there was something missing. I wasn't even sure I wanted to be out on my own. Where I'd once craved freedom and escape, now all I needed was the solace and security of the children's home. And I was very careful to do exactly as I'd been told. I went straight to the bakery, I did my work, and I came straight back again.

This was the new me, and I wanted no trouble at all. I earned £11 a week, which felt like a fortune. That first weekend, when my boss handed me a brown envelope with my wages inside, I felt a peculiar rush of satisfaction and shame. With the money in my hand, my mind flashed back to my mother's punters slapping five or 10 notes on the bedside table, when they had finished with her.

I remembered too the way Albert had pressed a coin into my hand, on his way out of the darkened bedroom. I was confused by the idea of accepting money, it felt somehow grubby and underhand, as though I had done something wrong. Yet at the same time, the concept of work was wholesome. I had done my job, and earned my pay, and I knew I ought to be pleased with myself.

"You did well," my boss smiled. "See you next Saturday."

A few Saturdays later, I was given permission to go to WHSmith after work, to spend my wages on a book.

"Here's our best customer," smiled the lady on the till, as she rang through my latest purchase in the *Sweet Valley High* series.

I loved that she knew me. I loved that someone took an interest in what I did and what I read. Here, in the new children's home, I felt, for the first time, as though I really mattered. One day, after work, I popped into the chemist on my way to the bus stop. I had no reason to go in there, and no conscious idea of what I might buy. But when I saw a child's dummy, hanging on a stand, I knew I had to have it.

"Is this for your baby brother or sister?" asked the chemist as she counted out my change.

"Yeah," I lied.

As soon as I got back to my bedroom, I unwrapped the dummy and popped it in my mouth. It was such a comfort. When I went down to dinner, I slipped it onto a ribbon around my neck.

"Didn't know you had a dummy?" Lara asked.

"I just fancied it," I replied. "I can't explain it."

Some of the other girls made jokey comments, but mainly they left me alone. The staff ignored it too. For me, having a dummy was not strictly about regression because I had never experienced this phase of my development in the first place. I'd never had a dummy. I'd never really had a childhood. I was a little mother myself when I was not much more than a toddler. I have often wondered, looking back, why I waited until I was happy and settled before I needed a dummy. But perhaps it was precisely because I was happy and settled that I now felt able to revisit my early years and go through the stages of life which I had missed.

There were two completely different sides to my character. On the one hand, I was streetwise, mature and grown-up. I was used to looking after myself and looking after younger ones too. And yet, in contradiction, I was also very young for my age. I loved cuddles and snuggles on the sofa. I liked to have my dummy around my neck. I loved the feeling of velvet too, between my fingers. It was like a comfort blanket to help me relax. When the sewing teacher heard, she gave me several squares of brightly coloured velvet. Each night, I had one waiting, with my dummy, on my pillow. Slowly, as my confidence grew, the toddler inside me receded, and the teenager stepped up into the limelight. And as part of my progress, I began taking lessons, in the big kitchen, with the cooks.

The cooks were like the characters I'd met in children's books; wholesome, pillowy and reassuringly maternal. They were everything I thought a mother should be. Even though I was still over-eating, and hoarding, I associated food with contentment and well-being, and I took every chance I could to help in the kitchen. One cook, Sharon, was soft-hearted and always cooked whatever I asked. If there was beef stew, and I didn't fancy it, she'd scrub out the menu and replace it with a beef curry. I could always talk her round to cooking one of her famous curries.

The second cook, Joan, was a huge lady with a beaming smile. The folds of fat around her face wobbled when she laughed, and we all felt it too. Joan cooked fry-ups for every single breakfast, and sometimes for dinner too. Pauline was the cook who gave me my lessons. She had grey hair, spectacles and endless patience. My first attempt at a spaghetti bolognese was a disaster, it was more like a lumpy soup.

"You mustn't give up," she told me, as I slopped it all into the bin. "You need practice, we'll cook again tomorrow."

By the time she'd finished with me, I could cook a roast dinner from scratch, a curry and bolognese. I baked cakes, biscuits and pies. Whenever Sally, the children's home manager, caught me in the kitchen, she chased me out.

"This is not a place for children," she admonished.

But as soon as she'd walked away, I'd sneak right back in. I loved perfecting my techniques. Yet my cookery lessons were less about skills, and more about love.

The kitchen cupboards were locked at night, but I could not resist creeping down the stairs, after bedtime, in search of food. I knew I was risking getting into trouble. But eating was a compulsion. Food was my friend, my only friend at certain times of my life, and we could never be apart for long. Besides, I'd been short of food for so much of my childhood, I never knew when the next enforced separation might be, and I could not help but stockpile, just in case.

My favourite was the biscuit cupboard. Sally had the keys to the cupboard and so I had to pick the lock, every time. The cooks had a delicious recipe for chocolate and caramel biscuits and contentment spread through me, like melting chocolate, after every bite. There were chest freezers in a room out the back too, and I'd help myself to frozen pies or puddings and then hide them in the garden, or in the bathroom, whilst they defrosted. I had food stashed all over the place; in the waste-paper bin, behind my bed, under the large stones in the garden. I was like a little squirrel, going from one outpost to another, checking on my supplies.

My wages, too, increasingly went on chocolate, instead of on books. My favourite treat was a Mars Bar. As soon as I was paid, on Saturday evening, I'd go straight to the shop and pick up maybe a dozen Mars Bars, stuffing three or four down my top whilst paying for the rest. On these occasions, I'd walk home instead of getting the bus, just to make it last longer. I savoured each delicious step, each heavenly mouthful. I made sure I took the long way round, meandering through the trees, so I could eat as much as I could.

That walk home was glorious. And even then, even when I was sick and bloated with over-eating, I wasn't satisfied. It was never enough. Never enough to fill the aching void inside. With so many calories, I realised, to my dismay, I was putting on weight. I'd always been a little overweight, but now, at nearly 14 years of age, I was around a dress size 14/16.

"I don't want to be fat," I told my social worker. "But I don't know what to do about it."

She, of course, did not know about my illicit Mars Bar frenzies. Nor did she know I often raided the kitchen cupboards and freezers in the middle of the night. She presumed, logically, I was being over-fed. After discussions, the staff reduced my portion sizes and tried to help me cut out snacks and sweets. But it was such a challenge.

"You've had plenty to eat," they told me after every meal. "You don't need chocolate. You can't have snacks."

But my eating was emotional, not physical. I always needed chocolate. Always. When I continued, inexplicably, to put weight on, it was decided I should try Weight Watchers. I was really pleased by the prospect, until the diet actually began. That first night, everyone in the dining room ate spaghetti carbonara and garlic bread and I was served a measly chicken salad. The portion was so small, I had finished it in a few bites.

"I can't live on this," I moaned. "It wouldn't fill a flea. I'll starve to death."

The cooks did their best to cheer me up, making me healthy meals and low-calorie snacks. I cut down on my Mars Bars binges and stolen treats from the kitchen. And slowly, the pounds rolled off. I was used to wearing jogging bottoms and sweatshirts all the time. But now, a couple of dress sizes smaller, Issy took me shopping and I chose new jeans and a size 12 off-the-shoulder gypsy top, with loose, frilled sleeves. It was so feminine and completely different from what I was used to. Lara wolf whistled when I showed her my new outfit.

"Hope, you look knock-out," she smiled.

I did a little twirl around my bedroom, before sinking back onto the bed.

"I feel much better than I did," I admitted. "The diet was a good idea, you know. Coming to this place has saved my life, Lara honestly. I just feel like it keeps getting better and better."

13

I FELT like a fortune-teller, as well as a matchmaker, when my social worker called me later that week.

"I've got good news, Hope," she said. "I'm coming to see you."

I couldn't wait. It had to be something important, for her to pay me a visit.

"Maybe she's found me a foster family," I said to Lara. "That would be the best news of all. I'd love foster parents, I really would. Just like Callum and Issy. I'd like the dad to be a policeman and the mum to be an aerobics instructor."

"I know," Lara said. "But you have to remember Hope, you're a teenager. It's unlikely you'll get a foster placement now. The older you get, the harder it is to find a family."

But I was already carried away, in my head, with fluffy daydreams of a strong, sensible police officer to keep me safe, and a glamorous aerobics instructor, with kind eyes and bouncing curls. We could snuggle up on the sofa, watch trash on telly, go shopping on Saturdays, dye our hair on Sundays. I pictured us painting each other's nails, her showing me how to apply my make-up, me picking her brains for my homework.

"It might happen," I told myself. "It just might."

My social worker dragged out the suspense by taking me out for a burger. Often, these trips out were tainted by bombshell news, and I was a bit wary as I placed my order. But this time, as I took a sip of my drink, she pushed a newspaper towards me.

"Open this and tell me if you recognise anyone inside," she said.

Mystified, I flicked through the pages, until part-way through, I shrieked loudly in amazement. The whole café turned and gawped, but I barely noticed. Because there, on the page, was a black and white photo of me, underneath the heading: 'Can you give this child a home?' It was a fostering advert. For me! My name had been changed, but there was a short write-up, listing my hobbies, reading, cooking and sewing. The article said I enjoyed school, especially history and craft.

"It makes me sound so clever," I laughed.

The social worker explained they were doing everything they could, going all out, to find me a foster family, once and for all.

"I won't let you down," I promised, seizing her hand. "I promise I won't. I'm going to behave myself really well. The foster parents will be impressed when they meet me. I mean it."

My social worker smiled.

"I'd really like a policeman and an aerobics instructor," I said, grinning, as my daydream took flight once again.

"But," I added hastily, "Obviously, anyone will do."

She smiled again.

"I'm on the case," she promised.

Back at the children's home, I adopted a new regime of behaviour which was religiously strict. I turned up early for work in case the foster parents wanted a reference from my boss. I stayed late, to help clean the shop, without extra wages.

"Hope, you've been absolutely brilliant today," my boss told me. "Here, take a couple of these chocolate cakes. My treat."

I shook my head.

"Thanks, but I'd rather not," I replied.

I had a good reason now to watch my weight. I reasoned prospective foster parents might prefer me if I was thin. Back at the children's home, I helped out where I could, especially in the kitchens. But there was no stealing, no hoarding of food. Absolutely no shoplifting. I didn't drink or take drugs. Usually, I never went anywhere without my trusty can of gas, but I threw it into a skip with a sense of purpose and without a single regret. Those days were well and truly behind me. I didn't want to give my foster parents a single reason to dislike me or doubt me. I had to prove myself. I had gone from being borderline delinquent to good as gold, from hell-raiser to people-pleaser. There was no middle ground, no balance between the two. Each time I was called to the office, my insides somersaulted, wondering if there was news from my social worker.

"Not yet, Hope," the staff told me. "Give it time."

At night, as I drifted off to sleep, I tried to visualise my new parents. Would he have a beard, the policeman? Fair hair, or dark? Dark, I hoped. And would my foster mum wear all that fluorescent gym gear? I wasn't so keen on that. I quite liked the idea of a mum I could cuddle up to. I wanted her to be thin, but not too skinny. I got so carried away with all the details, that I forgot these people existed only in my imagination.

"Slow down, Hope," I told myself.

But it was impossible. I was on an emotional bobsleigh run, gathering speed and enthusiasm, whizzing round each corner with such anticipation, it left me breathless.

And then, the call came.

"Hope, I've got news," my social worker announced. "I'm coming to see you."

She was trying to keep her voice neutral, but I could hear the excitement in her tone. I knew she had found me a family. I just knew it. We went to the same burger restaurant and, as we sat down, I couldn't take any more suspense.

"Did anyone come forward?" I spluttered. "Did anyone want me?"

My social worker smiled and my pulse began to race.

"We found a lovely couple called Deborah and Darren," she said. "They are really keen to meet you."

My eyes swam with tears. Deborah and Darren. Already, they sounded perfect. They were lovely names; warm and down to earth.

"Deborah, Darren and Hope," I said softly to myself. Yeah, Debs, Daz and Hope. Sounds good."

My social worker grinned.

"It gets better you know," she said. "Deborah is an aerobics instructor, and Darren is a fireman. It's an unbelievable coincidence."

My jaw dropped. Even for me, this was stretching reality.

"That's amazing," I laughed. "And a fireman, yes, brilliant, that's even better than a policeman. A fireman can keep me safe."

The social worker explained she'd met with Deborah and Darren, and they had already started decorating a bedroom for me, so I could see it when I visited.

"We'll arrange a meeting soon," she promised. "You can get to know them, they can get to know you. We'll take it slowly. Don't worry about a thing."

But I was not worried in the slightest. I felt like my heart was going to explode with pure joy on the drive back to the children's home. I couldn't wait to see my new bedroom, meet my new parents, start my new school. This was a fairytale. A real-life fairytale. So dreams did come true, after all.

14

IT WAS so difficult for me to concentrate on anything else, whilst I was waiting for a call from Deborah and Darren. I'd been told they might visit me at the children's home first, and then I'd go and see them at their place. As delighted as I was, there was a faint undercurrent of anxiety and trepidation.

"What if they don't like me?" I worried. "What if I'm too mouthy? What if they find out about me stealing Mars Bars? What if they think I'm too fat?"

I still carried a couple of stubborn pounds, despite my efforts to lose weight.

"Hope, will you stop fretting," Issy said. "You're beautiful, you're funny, you're clever. They will love you, just as I do. I know they will."

And that was another niggle. I was worried about how Callum and Issy would feel, now I'd found myself real foster parents. They had been wonderful stand-ins, after all. I could never truly express what that meant to me.

"It doesn't mean I love you any less," I told Issy. "You'll always be my first foster mum. I just need a forever family. You do understand, don't you?"

Issy smiled and smoothed my hair with her hand.

"I know that," she said gently. "You know I will always love you. It's important for you to have your own family and I'm really pleased for you. I just want you to stop looking for problems."

I did my best to calm down. My behaviour was so good, it wouldn't have been out of place in church. I didn't even dare crack a joke, or use a swear word, in case I upset anyone.

"Debs, Daz and Hope," I kept telling myself. "Debs, Daz and Hope."

It rolled off my tongue, just as though we were destined to be together. This was fate, I truly believed it. In my daydreams, I envisaged a pink bedroom, with a white dressing table with fancy curved legs. Along the dressing table was a row of bottles; perfumes, creams and make-up. On the bed was a row of cuddly toys. And on my bedside table was a photo of Debs, Daz and me. I didn't want a teenager's bedroom. In my fantasy, my ideal room was perhaps more suited to a nine or 10-year-old girl. I'd never had a little girl's bedroom, after all. I'd never had toys, or teddies, of my own. Before I was taken into care, I'd never even had a room of my own. Again, as with the dummy I used, and my velvet squares, there was a dichotomy between the wise-cracking, worldly, teenage face I showed each day, and the vulnerable little girl who hid beneath the surface. I wanted nothing more than my own bedroom, in my own home, where I could seize back some of the childhood I'd never had.

I began marking days off my calendar; a countdown, until the big day. I crossed off one week, then another. But the weeks turned into months, and I heard nothing. Even Callum and Issy seemed concerned. I turned 14, but I didn't want to celebrate. My mind was elsewhere. I wanted to spend my birthday with

Debs and Daz, at their house. At my house. The children's home staff tried to call my social worker but apparently, she had left her job, and it wasn't clear who, if anyone, had taken over her caseload.

"What do you mean she's left her job?" I demanded, my eyes shiny with angry tears. "Nobody told me."

"We've asked her manager to call us back," Callum told me. "We're doing our best, Hope. I'm sorry. It's complicated because you have two social workers, and the one dealing with your foster application has had to leave her role."

At night, my mind ran riot, catastrophising. Maybe Darren had had an accident at work, he was a fireman after all. Had Deborah been knocked down by a bus? Maybe they'd just lost my number, lost my address. Or maybe, probably, definitely – they had found someone else. Someone they preferred. The idea had been lurking in my thoughts, all along. I just hadn't wanted to acknowledge it, to make it real. But the more I thought of it, the more likely it seemed. They had found another girl who didn't swear or steal or sniff gas. They'd found another girl who didn't categorise men as 'punter or not'. They'd found another girl who, quite simply, was better than me. And that girl was now sleeping in my bedroom, eating my dinners and sitting on my sofa.

"No," I sobbed, clenching my fists under the duvet, burying my face in the pillow to hide my tears. "No!"

The pain scissored through me, carving me into pieces. I felt wretched. I felt so unloved. Deborah and Darren, my beloved aerobics instructor and fireman, my foster parents, did not want me. Nobody wanted me. They had simply joined the list. And it was all my own fault.

You are a little whore. You are a little slut. You are a little slag.

15

THE ANNUAL sports' day dawned bright and sunny and, underneath the layers of despair, I felt a buzz of excitement. For one day at least, I vowed to forget about Deborah and Darren. Forget about being fostered. Forget about finding a family. I ran outside, more interested in helping organise the races than actually taking part myself.

And it was then, whilst I was cheering Lara on in the sack race, that I heard a familiar voice calling my name. I turned around and saw Tiffany. She was two years older than me so had left the care system a few months earlier. We eyed each other warily. Truth was, she and I were not pals and never would be. I hadn't forgotten or forgiven the way she had bullied Lara and me.

"What are you doing here?" I asked.

"I'm back to watch sports day," she said. "I got married, didn't you hear? This is my husband, Dougie."

I stared at the man next to her and my jaw dropped.

"Wow! Like, actually married?" I gasped.

I couldn't deny I was impressed. Marriage was a fairytale. An impossible dream. It just didn't happen to girls like us.

Dougie was not quite Prince Charming, he was anything

from early-20s to mid-30s; an old man in my eyes. But he was fun and he made me laugh. He chased me too, into the trees at the end of the field, and tickled me until I cried with laughter. When I turned, I caught Tiffany glaring daggers at me and I felt a small thrill of satisfaction.

Serves you right for being a bully. No wonder your husband prefers me.

It got better too. When Dougie suggested I meet him, at Waterloo station, the following Friday, I was stunned.

"Course," I nodded, feeling slightly repulsed, but flattered too.

It was wrong, sneaking out to meet a man in London, I knew that. But I'd been doing the right thing for months now and where exactly had that got me? I'd been on my best behaviour, and still Deborah and Darren didn't want me. My own mother and father didn't want me. So yeah, if Dougie wanted to meet up, why not? The way I saw it, I had nothing left to lose.

That night, whilst everyone else was chatting about sports day, I thought only of Dougie and Tiffany and that shiny band on her ring finger which symbolised everything I'd ever dreamed of.

"Married," I said to myself.

The more I said it, the more I liked it. The more I wanted it to be me.

* * * *

The bigger part of me didn't believe for a moment Dougie would actually be under the clock, at Waterloo, as he had promised. Why would a man like him bother with a girl like me? Yet the small child inside of me still clung to the fantasy. In my pipe dream, Dougie was my way out of here, the answer to all my prayers. If I'd had an Aladdin's lamp, I'd have rubbed it, and wished for a man like Dougie to come to my rescue. The tragic irony of that fills me with sadness now. How could I be at once so shrewd and so astute, yet so pitifully gullible and naïve. Why were my expectations for myself so low? Why did I believe I deserved so little? As I planned my trip into London, I pictured Dougie, with his hair stuck down with too much gel and his lips glistening with too much saliva, and I felt a blast of repulsion, which I quickly dampened down. Momentarily, my mind flicked back to the girls at the unit, and the way Jonno took them out of the room, one by one, to be groomed and abused.

'That's not the same thing,' I told myself firmly. 'Dougie isn't like Jonno.' Again, I squashed the thought, like a tiresome beetle underfoot.

That Friday, the staff at the children's home had planned a day out to Brighton, and after we got back, late in the afternoon, the other girls would be collected by their families, or they would take the bus or train, and go home for the weekend. I reckoned that would be my best chance to slip off, unnoticed, to meet Dougie. Normally, I'd have been pleased at the idea of a trip to the seaside. We were allowed to buy either an ice cream or a drink, so I chose my favourite Fab ice-lolly, and then we had a walk along the grey pebbly beach, complaining as the sharp stones poked through our sandals.

"This beach is murder on my feet," Lara complained, rubbing her soles inside her flip-flops. "Why can't we go somewhere sandy? Eh? Why do we have to have a walk anyway? Who likes walking?"

"Yeah," I mumbled vaguely.

My thoughts were elsewhere all day, planning my bid for freedom and my new life with Dougie. I had no intention, once I got away, of ever coming back to the children's home. I was wearing my swimming costume, underneath a pair of purple dungarees, and though it wasn't especially warm or sunny, I braved a paddle with the other girls.

"Hey!" I yelled, as Lara kicked a wave my way, and it splashed my costume, soaking me through.

I hadn't even told Lara where I was going. I knew she'd be off home, to see her parents, as usual. It wasn't that I didn't trust her. Perhaps it was more that I didn't trust myself. The idea of leaving Lara behind was hard. I'd miss her, and I'd miss Callum and Issy too. Still, I reminded myself I could come back and visit once I was settled in my new life. Maybe I would come back and watch sports day, with my husband, just like Tiffany. I'd flaunt my ring and say things like: 'I'll have to check with my husband.'

I liked the sound of that.

I was still damp, under my dungarees, when the school bus arrived back at the children's home, at around 4pm. It was always chaos, coming back from a trip, and most of the girls hurried off to pack a weekend bag, ready for their visit home. The staff were usually shorthanded and distracted and so, straight off the coach, without even going upstairs to change, or grab so much as my toothbrush, I made a quick dash down the hallway, to a fire door at the back of the building. Within moments, I was outside again, scrambling through undergrowth, towards the woodland area which backed onto the grounds of the unit.

Underneath my dungarees, the grit from the beach was rubbing against my legs. And, as I scaled a low wall, I cursed myself for not at least bringing a towel or a change of clothes. I hadn't packed a thing. I had been so intent on running away, I hadn't really thought past that. In my mind, it had seemed somehow romantic to leave my old life behind, taking with me nothing but a soggy costume and a pair of dungarees.

My hair was damp too, and I tried to tease it back into place with my fingers. Even though my curls were fading, I was still really proud of my permed bob; it was just the thing for the summer of 1988. Idly, I wondered whether it was my new hairstyle that had caught Dougie's attention. I felt so special, to be picked out, from all the other girls. Nothing could heal the raw wound created by Deborah and Darren's rejection. But Dougie's interest did help to soothe the hurt, a little. I can remember now how full of hope and optimism I was, as I picked my way through the brambles. I know now also that my appeal had nothing at all to do with my hair, my dungarees, or my sports' day performance. I was broken and vulnerable. I was lost and scared. I was the perfect prey.

It was slow-going through the woods, but I guessed it was less risky than being spotted running up the main road. Again, I was hopelessly naïve to think the staff might be out looking for me, combing the countryside. I wanted to believe I was wanted. I told myself I'd be sorely missed. Yet deep down, I knew they were probably busy unloading the bus and sorting out the weekend pick-ups, and in all likelihood, they'd have no inkling I was even missing. At the station, it was easy enough to jump onto a train without paying. And as the fields and cottages became roads and housing estates, my smile grew wider and wider. The changing landscape seemed to mirror the change in my own life. My new start.

And even if Dougie wasn't there when I arrived, I was still so glad to be out, in the wide world, on a secret mission all of my own. Every Friday evening, most of the girls went to see their parents or relatives for the weekend. I hadn't seen my own parents since I was 13. I even had a court order in place preventing them knowing where I was. My mother didn't want to see me, and I didn't want to see her, or so I kept on telling myself. And so on Fridays, I was always left behind, with nowhere to go and nobody to call my own.

Throughout my time in the care system, I had met hundreds of different people; children, social workers, youth workers, psychiatrists, psychologists, doctors and teachers. Yet despite those numbers, or rather because of them, I didn't have anyone to call my own. There was no-one who really meant something to me, or me to them. Sure, Lara was my friend, but she went home each weekend to her own family. Callum and Issy loved me, but they had a home and a life together which didn't involve me. Now, at last, I had a purpose, I had someone who wanted to meet me, and be with me, and it gave me a warm feeling.

I had to get two trains, a journey of almost two hours, and when I finally arrived at Waterloo, my stomach was flipping with excitement. I strode out onto the concourse, hardly daring to lift my head, to check. But sure enough, there he was, right under the famous old clock, with its four faces. Again, the irony was lost on me. Next to him was Tiffany, stony-faced, and Trev. Tagging along behind Trev was a girl called Tammy, who looked about my age.

"I can't believe it, I can't believe you're here," I gabbled. "I didn't expect it."

"Now, would I let you down?" said Dougie, waggling his finger in mock annoyance. "Don't be daft. Course I'm here."

Off we went, on a bus, through the busy London streets. These were the streets of my childhood, the places where my memories were pinned and preserved. I felt soothed and reassured; I was coming home. And it was all thanks to Dougie. We got off the bus, next to a supermarket.

"I've heard you're a dab hand at shoplifting," Dougie told me, flicking a glance at Tiffany. "Nip in here Hope and bring us some dinner."

I was only too anxious to impress. Tammy and I ran into the shop, grabbing random items and stuffing them down our clothes, and I realised my dungarees had been the perfect choice after all. We emerged into the cool of the early evening, carrying broccoli, a bag of pasta, frozen chips, chocolate and beers. Tiffany had remained outside, and somehow the escapade not only united Tammy and I, but also pitted us against Tiffany. Tammy dissolved into helpless giggles as she tried to pull out a bag of pasta which was wedged in the leg of my dungarees, and we both fell into a heap on the pavement. When Tiffany tutted and rolled her eyes, Tammy and I just laughed some more.

"You two girls are good value," winked Dougie. "Come on, let's get back and have a few drinks. It's getting late."

Just around the corner, we came to a high-rise block, towering up into the clouds.

"Nineteenth floor," Dougie said. "Let's hope the fucking lift's been fixed today."

Just outside the main doors was a red phone box. We walked past the phone box, into the foyer and then we bunched up in the lift, which stank of concentrated urine as it cranked slowly up the floors.

"This place makes me think of Towering Inferno," I told Tammy. "That film. Know what I mean? It's just so tall."

She nodded in eager agreement, though I wasn't sure she knew what I was talking about. I recognised in her a little bit of myself; a desperation to please, to be accepted and liked. And it was just like me to link everything with a film or a book, taking every chance I could to escape from reality. What I didn't realise was my choice of disaster movie was more apt than I could ever have imagined.

The flat itself, when we went inside, was sparsely furnished and smelly. The place was reminiscent of my childhood home, though not nearly as squalid. Still, I'd got used to the children's home, good furniture and regular cleaning, and my first thought was I didn't fancy putting my bare feet on this sticky floor. Not one bit. I certainly didn't want to have to use the bathroom. But all my misgivings were quickly swept aside by my elation at just being there. This was it. This was where I was going to live. This was my new life. I could cope with a sticky floor and a worn-out sofa. I ran to a window and peered out, through the stains and the smears, through the smog and the miserable grey clouds. Far below, though the light was fading, I could see dots of cars and specks of people.

"I feel like Rapunzel," I laughed. "I'm locked in my tower. Who will rescue me?"

Dougie slapped my bottom roguishly and I giggled.

"Shut up you silly cow, and smoke this," he said, handing me a joint. "I'm here. I've rescued you. Panic over."

I sank back onto the sofa, all hygiene concerns forgotten.

Dougie cracked open a can of Tennent's Extra for each of us, and then he flicked on the telly. He snuggled up in between Tammy and me, with Trev on the other side of Tammy. Tiffany glowered at Dougie. There was no room for her on the sofa. From being a dubious item of furniture the sofa suddenly became the place to be. I had no desire to move at all.

"What about me?" she hissed. "I'm your wife. What about me, Doug?"

"What about you, Tiff?" he laughed, as though it was a great punchline. His eyes were fixed on the telly, but his arm was tight around my bare shoulder, and I was conscious I was wearing only a swimming costume under my dungarees. He and Tiffany continued sniping, until Dougie suddenly said:

"Tell you what, Tiff. What about you piss off out and leave us to it. Okay?"

Even though Dougie framed it as a question, we all knew that was the end of the matter. The door slammed and, with a few expletives, she was gone. I experienced a fleeting moment of remorse, worrying about Tiffany, before reminding myself she hadn't worried too much about me when she was bullying me in the breakfast queue. And I was sure Tiffany was quite capable of looking after herself; she had, after all, achieved the impossible, by getting married after leaving the care system. I envied her, and I felt slightly in awe of her, but in truth, and I am ashamed to admit it now, I did not fret too much about her wellbeing.

I was a child; she was an adult. I did not think it was my place to look out for her. Besides, it was so cool at Dougie's flat. I was having the time of my life. He let us smoke and drink. He let us cook. He let us do just as we pleased. I boiled up some pasta and

Tammy stuck the chips in the oven. It was a strange carb-heavy combination, but I was thrilled just to be given the freedom of the greasy little kitchen. I wanted to show off all my cooking skills, even if it was just simple stuff. And by the time the pasta was drained, we were all quite drunk and stoned, so the meal didn't seem that unusual after all.

"Tasty this," Dougie said, with a mouthful of chips, and Tammy and I smiled and basked in the warmth of his praise.

At some point, in a drugged-up haze, I was aware of Tiffany coming back and hammering on the front door. She and Dougie had another row, before he got rid of her and locked the door to the living room. As he slid the bolt into place, she yelled one last insult, and Dougie threw back his head back and laughed. I could see an uneven row of black fillings at the back of his mouth, and a shudder ran through me.

"Don't look so serious, I'm locking her out, not locking you in," he said.

"Like Rapunzel," I slurred. "Like the fairytale. I'm locked away. Waiting for my prince."

I didn't exactly feel safe with Dougie, but then, I was used to feeling unsafe. And I was pleased to be there, nonetheless. He displayed, after all, the characteristics I had been conditioned to expect in a man; loud, cocksure, confident, with overtly sexualised behaviours. Later, he and Trev pulled the sofa out into a big bed, and we all climbed in together. There were lots of giggles and cuddles and messing about. I felt Dougie's arms around me, and he planted a light kiss on the back of my neck. It was a kiss goodnight; nothing more. And that was as far as it went. As I drifted off to sleep, I congratulated myself on having made the break, and fallen so lucky in my new life.

16

THE NEXT morning, Dougie gave us free run of the kitchen again. I boiled some pasta for breakfast, as it was all we had, and Dougie lit another joint.

"You're starting early," I smiled.

"Hey, it's never too early," he winked, and he handed me the spliff.

Again, I was blown away by my own good fortune. Dougie was nothing like the adults I'd come across in the children's homes and the secure units over the last few years. He was perfectly happy for me to drink and take drugs. He even provided them! And for free! This was better than I had even imagined.

"I'm never going back to the home again," I told him. "Never."

"That's okay," he smiled. "You can stay here, as long as you like."

There was no sign of Tiffany all that morning and again, any brief feelings of guilt or worry soon floated away in a woolly cloud of cannabis. Besides, I wasn't doing anything wrong. Dougie wanted me here, it was his place, and his decision. By late afternoon, we were all ravenously hungry and couldn't face yet another bowl of pasta.

"Come on girls, let's go shopping," Dougie said. "You two can pick up some food for us."

I didn't really feel like it, but I also sensed Dougie was not the sort of man to argue with. It was busy outside, a bustling Saturday tea-time, and I was suddenly aware I was still wearing my swimming costume and my dungarees. I hadn't had a wash or brushed my hair. And I was staggering a little too; tipsy and stoned, and squinting in the too-bright sunshine.

I didn't see the police officers until the last minute, they seemed to be upon us, from nowhere. Dougie and Trev must have been a few steps behind because they dissolved, like ghosts, into the crowd, and when I turned around, they had both vanished. In fact, when I thought about it, I wasn't sure they had even followed us out of the foyer in the flats.

"What are you two girls up to?" asked one of the officers. "Have you been drinking? Names? Addresses? Dates of birth?"

I started to laugh and crack jokes; my first line of defence.

"Rapunzel," I replied. "Aged 300."

Minutes later we were in the back of a police car, on our way to the station. We were shown into a small room, and I thought we'd been forgotten about until Sally, the boss from the children's home, stuck her angry face around the doorway. Tammy was in care too, but in a different children's home. A social worker arrived to collect her too.

"Honestly, Hope," Sally said. "We've been worried sick. You can't just take off like that. You're in real trouble you know."

I sulked all the way back. My new beginning, my great escape, had fallen apart on the second day. It was so pathetically childish, so badly planned out. I was furious with myself. The effects of the lager and the weed lingered, and a part of me was still back there, in the flat. I remembered looking out of the window and feeling so impossibly high.

I clung to those feelings of liberation and escape. I could see Dougie too, in my mind's eye, winking and laughing. I was missing it all already. And I was determined to go back. I would not give up, I told myself, no matter what punishments they threw at me.

"Early bedtimes for a week, and you're grounded for a month," Sally said, as we turned off the motorway. "You're going right to the bottom of the status chart."

"Yeah, yeah," I said, injecting as much derision into my tone as I could.

Back at the children's home, I threw myself on my bed, with a heavy heart. I wasn't sure how I'd be able to get in contact with Dougie again. I couldn't even remember exactly where he lived. All I knew was it was a block of flats, a bus ride away from Waterloo. But the next evening, one of the girls shouted me over to the phone, which was in the main corridor.

"Call for you, Hope," she yelled.

"Me?" I asked, surprised.

I didn't get calls. My parents didn't have my number, and my brothers were moving around different areas of the country. It was hard for us to keep in contact. Apart from the occasional call from Marie, who preferred to write or to visit, I didn't hear from anyone. Curiously, I picked up the receiver, and was astonished to hear Dougie on the other end.

"Alright?" he asked, chirpy as ever.

I imagined his eyes dancing with mischief, and I felt the thrill of insubordination.

"How did you get through here?" I asked admiringly.

It wasn't an external phone, and calls had to be approved by a staff member before they were put through.

"Never you mind," Dougie laughed.

His mysterious control over the phone system only added to his appeal, and I laughed too.

"Anyway," he continued. "You should be worrying more about staying out of the way of them cops. You just let 'em lift you the other day. I was watching out the window. Thought you'd do better than that."

So I had been right. It seemed he hadn't even left the flats; he'd just watched it all unfold from the safety of the tower block. Secretly, I'd been a bit hurt, the way Dougie had just left me to it to handle the police. But, I decided, there was no point in us all getting into trouble.

"You didn't tell the cops anything did you?" he pressed. "My name or address, nothing like that?"

"Course not," I replied, offended. "What do you take me for? I don't even know your last name, and I can't remember where the flat was. I wouldn't do that, anyway. You can trust me."

Truth was, the police hadn't even asked where I'd been, or who I'd been with. The officers had seemed irritated and put-out, impatient to get me out of the station and out of the way. The children's home staff hadn't asked me either. Sally was keen only to deliver punishments.

Dougie let out a long breath, and I could tell he was smoking. I was desperate for a cigarette myself. A nice can of cold lager maybe. I was almost 15 and yet, I was fast realising, the staff treated us like small children. I had weeks of early bedtimes to look forward to. I wasn't even allowed out to the shop on my own. My only small sliver of freedom, each week, was my job at the bakery. I was 14, yet I might as well have been four.

"Listen," Dougie said. "I haven't got long, I'm in the phone box. But I'll see you Friday, about six, under the clock. Alright?"

I put the phone down and my heart leapt. I had a second chance! I would not mess this up. No way.

"Who was that?" Lara asked, as I walked back down the corridor. "You got a boyfriend?"

"Maybe," I grinned.

I couldn't keep it to myself any longer.

"Wow, Hope," she said, when I'd finished. "You sure you know what you're doing?"

I nodded.

"He's really nice," I told her. "He bought me some lagers. He's got loads of weed. He lets me do what I want."

We were all in the same predicament, all looking for ways to survive, ways to escape. I knew Lara and the other girls would look out for me, just as I did for them. It was a collaborative effort, staying out of trouble. I wasn't the only one with a boyfriend either. I wasn't the only one who disappeared sometimes. We all had our secrets. We all had coping mechanisms.

"This is my way out of here," I added. And Lara understood.

Just like the previous week, I waited until everyone was busy, packing bags and arranging transport for their weekends at home. Taking nothing, I sprinted down the corridor, out through the fire door, and into the woodland. The fresh air was intoxicating. It smelled like freedom. I ran all the way to the train station, my heart racing with the combined effects of exercise and excitement. Today, I knew he'd be there. I just couldn't wait.

"Don't blow it, this time," I told myself. "No silliness. No getting yourself in trouble. Play it cool."

Dougie met me under the clock at Waterloo, as we'd agreed, and we took the bus back to his place, as before.

"Where's Tiffany?" I asked.

"Don't you worry about her," Dougie said, in a lazy way, as though she was of no consequence whatsoever. "Trev's gonna be along later, with young Tammy. But Tiff's not your problem. Understand?"

I smiled and nodded. I understood perfectly – or at least I thought I did.

In the flat, it didn't look like anyone had cleaned up since the previous weekend. There were empty cans on the floor, ashtrays spilling over, and a big spliff burn in the arm of the sofa. The place stank too. I was itching to open a window and throw the cans in the bin. But I didn't want to do anything to make Dougie like me any less. If he was happy to live in a tip, then I was too.

Dougie cracked open two cans, flicked on the telly, and sat on the couch. I sat down next to him with my legs curled under me, as though it was the most natural thing in the world. Maybe, I told myself, Dougie might have a friend, another gem, just like him, who might agree to marry me, after I left the children's home. It had happened for Tiffany, hadn't it? So why couldn't it happen for me? In the evening, Dougie went out to get more alcohol and a bag of crisps each.

"You'd best stay indoors," he laughed. "You're a wanted woman."

It was the first time anyone had ever called me a woman, aged 14, and I liked the sound of it. Dougie was the only person I knew who really took me seriously. Back in the flat, it seemed

113

to me like a scene of perfect domesticity; I tidied up whilst Dougie put the lagers in the fridge. I opened the crisps, and we had a handful each. Then we both snuggled up on the sofa, me scrolling through the TV channels whilst Dougie rolled a joint.

Later, clouded by drugs and drink, I curled up with him on the pull-out bed, his arms warm and comforting around me. We were so high up in the flat that I felt physically and emotionally out of reach. It was a bit like being on a different planet altogether. I felt safe, secure, untouchable. Looking back, I want to shake some sense into my teenage self, I want to yell at her to sit up and listen to the truth. I was holed up with a man who posed a greater threat to my safety than anyone I'd ever met. It was all well and good, keeping the rest of the world out, on the 19th floor. But it wasn't the rest of the world that I needed to fear. I was in there with the enemy himself. At 14, of course, I understood none of this. I turned in my sleep and half-smiled as Dougie's arm tightened around me. I felt as though, finally, I had someone who understood me.

"Night princess," he murmured, and my heart soared.

I marvelled at how in tune we were. It was as though he sensed I was looking for my very own fairytale ending. My very own prince. The next day, Dougie was awake before me.

"Come on, Hope," he said, ruffling my hair. "I've got a bit of business. I need you to disappear."

"Where? Why?" I stuttered. "What did I do wrong? I thought I could stay with you forever."

Dougie smiled.

"Listen, we can't be together until you leave the children's home. You know that. They'll just come looking for you, every time. Best you keep going back there, keep 'em happy, eh?"

HOPE DANIELS

I nodded dejectedly.

"You and me princess, we're going to be together forever," Dougie promised. "Tiff is gone. I promise you. I'm waiting for you."

He leaned forward and planted a kiss on my forehead.

"Happy now?" he asked.

Again, I nodded. I even managed a smile.

'You and me princess, we're going to be together forever.'

The journey back to the train station passed in a blur, and it was nothing to do with drugs. I could have floated back to the children's home, on my own cloud nine, without the need for public transport. Dougie, I realised, was the perfect gentleman; he was doing everything the right way. It made absolute sense; if I ran away for too long, I'd end up back in a secure unit, and I'd never see him again. It was so important to take things steadily and sensibly. The staff at the home were waiting when I got back, and predictably they were furious about my disappearance.

"You're supposed to be grounded! You've lost points on the status chart," they told me. "There's a movie night and a takeaway next week. You're banned."

I smiled sweetly. I didn't care one bit. Dougie and I were going to be together. Forever. I didn't need to watch movies. I was living in dreamland.

17

SOMEHOW, DOUGIE managed to get through on the communal phone a few days later, so we could make our arrangements to meet up again. By now, the staff were wise to me running away on Fridays and they were watching me all of the time. But I just relished the challenge to get one over on them.

"I've had a good think about this," I told Dougie, in a whisper. "It's no use me trying to get out of here on Friday, they're expecting it. I'm not allowed out at all during the week, but I'm working on Saturday. I could leave work a bit early and come and meet you then?"

"Working?" scoffed Dougie. "Didn't know you had a job. Bloody hell."

It was odd, I thought, how little we knew about each other, yet how serious we were. I wanted to spend the rest of my life with Dougie, but I didn't even know his last name. I didn't know anything about him, except he was married to Tiffany, and I didn't like to dwell on that. We agreed I would try and get away from work half-an-hour or so early. That way, I could be on the train to London by the time the staff found out I was missing.

"Yeah, sounds like a plan," Dougie said.

That Saturday, I made up a fib to my boss about needing to

leave early for an appointment and then, I was off. It was all so easy. I arrived at Waterloo a little earlier than arranged, and I wandered around, amongst the strangers, the hustle and bustle, wondering where they were all going and what they were all doing, to necessitate such a rush. All these people seemed to be so pressed for time. Yet I had all the time in the world. Most of them were probably in London to make a fortune, to make a statement, to announce themselves. I was in London to hide, to lose myself, to disappear behind the advertising hoardings and slip through the pavement cracks. Even now, although I had Dougie, I felt marginalised and excluded; marked out. Being in the care system was like a dull cramp. A lesion; always there, always painful, no matter how I tried to hide it.

When I finally spotted Dougie, striding across the station concourse, my heart sank. He was with Tiffany, who gave me daggers across the crowd. And as she got nearer, I noticed, with a jolt, that she was cupping a slight bump in her belly. I couldn't take my eyes off it.

"First prize," she said sarcastically. "You worked it out, well done. I'm pregnant."

"Not now, Tiff," said Dougie sharply.

I didn't speak all the way back to the flat. My mind was churning. If it was Dougie's baby, how on earth could he be with me? That didn't seem right. When we arrived, Dougie handed me the door key.

"You go on up princess," he said. "I just need a quick word with Tiff. She's off to see her pal today. That's right Tiff, isn't it?"

She scowled but I took no notice. It was some comfort to have Dougie's door key in my hand. A vote of confidence. Of ownership. I felt that counted for something, at least. And it wasn't long before Dougie followed me up, alone.

"What's going to happen about Tiffany?" I asked him. "She's having a baby, isn't she? And you're her husband. Is it your baby? I don't want to be in the way."

Already, I felt I'd said too much, and Dougie pressed his finger onto my lips.

"Sshh," he said. "Don't you worry about Tiff. I'll sort her out. She's got what she wanted – she's got a baby. Her and me are done.

"Like I told you, as soon as you're out of that place, you and me are gonna to be together. Tiff is history. I promise you that, princess."

I wanted to believe him. I needed to believe him. And so, I did. I was adept at seeing only what I wanted to see; it was a survival technique. When I was little, I told myself the shop-keepers were nasty, to justify my stealing. I told myself Dad was tired and sad and that was why he was always drunk. Everyone around me lied to me, and so, I lied to myself. I believed Dougie when he said we'd be together. Besides, I was a child. Dougie was a grown man. I trusted him, I was a little in awe of him too. I was even rather frightened of him.

I had been raised to let men dominate and bully, especially in relationships. And to me, this was a relationship. I was having an affair, a secret affair, an adulterous affair, with Tiffany's husband. Whenever my thoughts ran away with me like that, I became paralysed by guilt. I was rotten, through and through. Despite Tiffany's behaviour towards me, she didn't deserve this. When I was alone in the children's home, I thought of her and Dougie, in their flat, snuggling up on the same sofa which I shared with him, and the shame ate away at me. I despised myself. But I was jealous too. I wanted what she had. And the more time I spent with Dougie, the more I invested in him, and the less I thought about Tiffany. She was like a tide going out, receding further and further into the distance, until she was no more than a thin, hazy line on the horizon.

"Hope, I'm gonna marry you," Dougie told me. "I'm serious. I wanna be with you."

A flower bloomed in my chest as he spoke.

"Really?" I said.

A wedding! I was actually going to get married! Guiltily, I thought of Simon Le Bon. I had been so set on marrying him. I had declared undying love for him. But Dougie was here, Dougie was real. Dougie wanted me.

"I want to be with you too," I told him.

My imagination went into overdrive, and I wondered if we might be able to have a big white wedding, with all the trimmings, just like I'd always dreamed. I saw myself in a big white dress, with a long, floaty train. I wanted a veil, and a sparkling tiara. Six bridesmaids, all in powder-pink dresses, and two cute little pageboys. I fancied a horse and carriage to take me to church, and a Rolls-Royce with a chauffeur to drive us to the airport for our honeymoon. It would be somewhere exotic, though I hadn't really thought that far ahead. I'd always dreamed of an archway of white flowers and balloons outside the reception hotel, where we could pose for photos. I wanted to ask Dougie if he'd carry me over the threshold, into our new home. I'd seen that in films. It was so romantic. We needed to talk about florists, chauffeurs and photographers. And what about a vicar? I started making a wedding list, inside my head.

Would I wear white, or ivory? And what sort of wedding rings would we choose? I loved white gold. The fantasy played like a film reel, inside in my head, but then it jammed, and I was spun all the way back to the reality of Dougie's dingy flat.

All this was way off, into the future, I reminded myself sharply. Best not to bother Dougie with it. I might get on his nerves, prattling on about the wedding. He might even change his mind and stay married to Tiffany! That was another thing to add to my list, he'd need to get divorced. No, it wasn't something to mention just yet. And so, I kept all my plans and my dreams to myself. Deep down, in the centre of my soul, perhaps I understood this was nothing more than a tragically misguided daydream. Perhaps I stayed silent because I was so scared of breaking the spell.

My visit to Dougie's, like the previous one, lasted overnight. He held my hand as we nestled on the sofa. He cuddled me as we went to sleep. When it was time for me to go back to the children's home, he took me in his arms.

"Hope, I love you," he murmured. "I'll see you next week. My little princess."

I skipped down the stairs, without waiting for the lift.

He loves me, he loves me, he loves me!

The announcement flashed, in pink neon across my eye-line, bouncing off every wall, off every passing bus, off every street sign. I had someone who loved me! At last! Never mind Deborah and Darren. Never mind my own feckless parents. I had Dougie now. My Dougie. I couldn't wait to see him again. Back at the children's home, I didn't care what my punishments were. None of the staff asked where I had been, or who I'd been with. They were concerned only about me making a nuisance of myself.

Taking up valuable time and resources. I was not worth it, and I knew that, only too well. Marie, my old teacher, called, and I suspected the staff had asked her to intervene.

"I heard you've been running away, getting into trouble," she said. "Is there anything I can help with? Anything you want to tell me?"

"No," I said shortly.

I loved Marie, but I wasn't about to confide in her. I was beyond all that. She could never have understood. The next Friday, a residential worker was assigned to keep an eye on me, and I just couldn't get away. I cursed as the clock ticked by, and the last train to Waterloo left the local station, without me on it. I pictured Dougie standing under the clock, looking for me. Looking for the girl he loved. Late that night, I was called to the phone.

"Where were you?" Dougie demanded.

"Couldn't get away," I whispered. "This place is like a prison. I'll try again tomorrow."

"Tell you what, I'll come and see you tomorrow," he replied. "I'll be in the woods, behind the field, at around 7pm."

I couldn't sleep that night. And the next day, all I could think of was Dougie. The idea of him being so close to the children's home was electrifying. It was a big risk, sure. But it was one he was prepared to take, for my sake. It wasn't difficult to slip away in the evening. The staff were more relaxed after dinner. I only needed to tell a small fib about having a headache, which brought the desired reaction from the duty manager.

"Have a walk around the garden," she said. "Fresh air usually helps a headache."

I smiled gleefully and slipped out of the back door. The

victory felt even sweeter, now the staff themselves had given me my way out.

"Won't be long," I promised.

Dougie was waiting in the woods. As I reached him, he took me by the shoulders and pushed me up against a tree. He kissed me so forcibly; it startled me. I wasn't sure I liked having a tongue poking into my mouth. It was the first time I'd ever had it. But I told myself, this was what happened in films and books. This was what growing up was all about. And it was another sure sign that he really liked me. It was my 15th birthday later that week too. Another milestone, another step closer to Dougie and me being together.

"It's my birthday the day after tomorrow," I told Dougie, when he paused for a break in kissing.

But Dougie didn't seem to hear me.

"God, I've missed you," he groaned, kissing me again, pulling my hair back from my face.

He had brought a four-pack of lager, and we had one each, before he ushered me back towards the building.

"We don't want anyone coming out looking for you," he said. "I'm thinking of you, princess. Don't want you getting into trouble, that's all."

But as I let myself back in, through the back door, two staff members, Freda and Mia, were waiting.

"Hope, where have you been?" Freda asked. "You went for a walk round the garden nearly an hour ago."

"And you've been drinking," Mia said accusingly. "I can smell it on you. Get upstairs, and we'll deal with this tomorrow."

I rolled my eyes. This was ridiculous. I'd had a can of lager, so what? I laughed to myself, imagining how much they'd overreact if they knew where I had really been. I was prepared for the usual punishments, the early bedtimes, the lack of treats. I didn't give a damn what they threw at me. Nobody here cared about me. Deborah and Darren didn't care. My own family didn't care. Dougie was all I had. I wanted to feel pleased and smug and loved up, as I climbed into bed. Instead, I felt anxious and lonely and confused.

18

"HOPE!" SALLY called across the dining room. "Straight into the office after breakfast please."

"OK," I replied, my mouth full of cornflakes.

This was odd. I felt my mood dip a little.

"Good luck," Lara said, as I carried my dish back to the kitchen. "Wonder what they want you for?"

I shrugged, trying to look like I wasn't bothered. But it wasn't usual to be ordered into the office. I knew this was about more than just another punishment. I took a seat in the office and Sally swivelled around on her office chair to face me. She was strict and hardline at the best of times, but today her face was set like concrete. Her mouth was pulled tightly together as though by drawstrings, each deep wrinkle like a pleat in her skin. If she'd ever smiled, I'd never seen it.

"Hope, we've decided to move you upstairs to a new unit," she said. "You've had lots of chances, but you just keep absconding. We need to know where you are. We have to keep you safe."

I stared at her, horrified.

"Are you joking?" I stammered.

The upstairs unit was known as the semi-independent unit. There were more rules up there and a lot less fun. Girls were encouraged to look after themselves; to learn to cook, clean and wash. They were expected to attend classes and complete tasks without support. It was ironic that at the point in my life when I needed the most help, I was being cut loose. I desperately needed guidance and advice from the people who knew and loved me. So they were moving to a place where I knew nobody.

Upstairs, the staff were different. The girls were different. Even though the units were connected, we didn't see the girls from upstairs at all, expect at mealtimes and even then, it was strictly segregated.

"What about Lara?" I demanded. "What about my mates?"

"You won't be permitted to come back down to this unit for any reason," Sally replied. "You're moving upstairs and that's the end of it. We feel you need a fresh start, away from here."

My head fell forwards, into my hands, as I tried to hold back my tears. Through my fingers, I saw Callum passing the office. I could tell, from his face, he already knew. In time-honoured tradition, everyone knew except me. It was too cruel.

"How could you?" I sobbed. "You're supposed to be my foster dad! Now you're getting rid of me!"

Everyone got rid of me, eventually. I never lasted long, as a daughter, a pupil, a friend. Always, always, I got moved on.

I am a little slut, I am a little whore, I am a little slag. I am infected.

Callum frowned and sighed.

"It's for the best," he said sadly.

How could that possibly be true? I marched past him, burning up with fury and resentment. I was angry with all the staff, but especially so, irrationally so, with Callum and Issy. I had trusted them, loved them, adopted them as my own. They were supposed to fight for me. Instead, they had let me go. They had let me down.

Upstairs, I threw myself on my bed, in my strange new room, and I cried. I didn't come out for dinner. And the next morning, as my 15th birthday dawned, I didn't even come down to breakfast. There was a small pang of regret as I wondered whether the cooks had baked me a birthday cake. Their cakes were legendary. But I had no interest in birthdays, or in cakes. I preferred to stay in bed and wallow in furious self-pity all day. Late in the afternoon, I found a few wrapped presents outside my door, alongside a plate of snacks.

"I am not hungry!" I yelled down the empty corridor, in the vain hope anyone was listening.

For weeks, I had been pestering Issy for a must-have Athena poster; an image of a man holding a baby in his arms. It was an iconic '80s picture and most girls my age had it on their bedroom wall. I liked it especially because the man looked so gentle and tender. The complete antithesis from all the men I'd ever met. As I unwrapped my presents, the poster unfurled out of a long tube. But I could barely look at it. They had sold me out, completely. And all I could see, in the poster, was a frightened baby, an infant who needed to feel safe, and didn't. I didn't even put the poster on the wall. I couldn't bear the reminder of what it stood for. Sullenly, I shoved it under the bed and tried to forget about it. Even now, fast-forward almost 35 years, I can't look at that poster without feeling sick.

The day after my birthday, I gave in to my hunger and went down to breakfast. All the units shared the same dining room, so it would at least be a chance for me to see Lara and my friends briefly. I didn't want to see any of the old staff. I felt so betrayed.

"Oh Hope, I can't believe it," Lara said, as we queued in line with everyone else, for orange juice. "I'm gonna miss you so much."

"Me too," I said miserably.

There were two long tables in the dining room, one for the downstairs girls, and one for the upstairs girls. I was not allowed to sit with my old friends or the old staff. Instead, I had to sit opposite on the new table, and watch, enviously, as they chatted and laughed. I saw Lara nick a slice of toast off another girl's plate, in that easy way that friends have, and a wave of sadness enveloped me. It was agony, sitting here, looking in at my old life.

Here's what you could have had, Hope. But you blew it again. And it's all your own fault.

That was the worst of it. Much as I railed against Sally, against Callum and Issy, I knew I was to blame. I felt too despairing, too desolate, to eat a thing and I slopped my cereal into the bin before stacking my bowl and cutlery. As we were walking out of the dining room, Lara caught up with me and whispered: "You got a call last night. I took it for you. You've to meet Dougie on Friday, usual time and place. Under the clock. That make sense?"

I felt a sudden frisson of excitement. Trust Dougie to find a way to get through to me. I felt like a member of the French resistance, receiving coded messages in an unsuspecting crowd.

"Thanks," I whispered. "I feel like an undercover agent."

We both laughed and then, my name was called, and I was ushered back upstairs. That was what hurt most about the move to the new unit. There was nobody for me to laugh with. Nobody for me to be myself with.

I knew it would be hard to get away that Friday. But I also

knew nothing would stop me. My plan was to leave earlier than usual before the staff were expecting it. I excused myself out of English, the last lesson of the day, saying I needed the toilet. Instead, I ran past the bathroom, down the stairs, and through the corridor. Within minutes, I was running through woodland, brambles scratching at my skin, and not caring one bit. We went straight to the flat. When we got inside, Dougie wanted to know why I hadn't been around to take his call.

"I've been moved upstairs," I explained. "Because I keep running away. There's a phone in the new place too but I don't know if you'll be able to get through."

"I'm sure I will," Dougie said, with the air of a man who was used to getting his own way.

I was bursting to say more. I wanted to tell him about my rotten birthday, spent sobbing in my bed, in my new unfriendly room. I wanted to tell him about my Athena poster, lying crumpled under my bed. But I sensed somehow Dougie wouldn't want to hear about that. He didn't seem to have even remembered my birthday; he made no mention of it. And the children's home was another world, completely. Now I was with Dougie, smoking drugs and drinking special brew, my other life seemed so terribly tame and childish.

"I thought we'd have a bit of a session, me and you," Dougie grinned.

"Brilliant," I replied.

I meant it too. I was up for anything to give me a break from my own thoughts. Rifling through Dougie's CD collection, as I smoked a joint, I asked him:

"Do you have any Duran Duran? Do you like Simon Le Bon?"

Dougie threw his head back and laughed, though I didn't see what was funny. Again, I saw his black fillings glinting as they caught the sunlight which streamed through the streaks on his windows.

"Here," he said, handing me a can of strong lager. "Get this down you. I've got plans for you this afternoon, princess. And no, I don't like Duran fucking Duran."

Trev and Tammy arrived, and Dougie turned the music up loud.

"Come on girls, have a dance," he said, pushing the sofa back against the wall. There wasn't much other furniture, so there was plenty of space. He opened the door to a second room too, which probably should have been a bedroom, but was instead completely empty. As the drugs and booze took hold, Tammy and I laughed and twirled our way around the flat. I felt good at first. Full of fun. The lager was a gentle anaesthetic, dumbing my reality down, pushing my problems right to the furthest corners of my mind. But as the afternoon wore on, I started to feel sickly and foggy; slurry and muddled. I couldn't make myself understood.

"I feel bad," I tried to tell Dougie, but he just smiled lazily.

Tammy was flaked out, on the edge of the sofa.

"Come here," Dougie told me, as I staggered a little.

He slipped an arm around my waist, almost carrying me into the empty room. There were black spots in my vision. The walls were wavy, dancing towards me and back, then vanishing completely. I felt myself slipping away and then lurching back again, as though I was on a big, scary swing.

"Steady now," Dougie said, as he laid me down on the floor-boards.

The next thing I knew, I was stumbling into the lift, jabbing at all the buttons. My thoughts were crashing, in one big pile-up, and I didn't know why I was running or who I was running from. I just knew I had to get away. Tears streamed down my face as the lift clanked to a halt, and I rushed outside, the fresh air smacking at my face like a shot of adrenaline. I was immediately more alert. The red phone box, just outside the block, was mercifully empty. I fell inside and called the children's home, reversing the charges.

"Please come and pick me up," I sobbed. "I don't know what I'm doing. I need some help."

I didn't even know who I'd spoken with or if they'd understood me. Slumped on the floor of the phone box, I waited in a daze, until a car pulled up, with one of the residential workers inside. I couldn't remember having told him where I was. Perhaps he'd worked it out from the phone box number. Dougie hadn't followed me outside and I was too spaced out to realise or to care.

"Hope, how the hell have you got yourself in such a state? What have you taken?" asked the residential worker, on the long drive back. "Why do you keep running away? Why do you never learn?"

I shrugged, leaning my forehead against the cool glass of the car window, and closing my eyes. The effects of the drugs lifted slowly as we drove, but my mind was still shrouded in foggy uncertainty. I didn't want to answer any of his questions. Truth was, I didn't know the answers, anyway.

19

AS I was cleaning my teeth in the bathroom later that same night, one of the girls exclaimed:

"That is a whopper, Hope. Who gave you that?"

The others clustered around to look at a love bite on my neck. I had another on my chest too. They were only visible now I'd taken off my hoodie and put my pyjamas on.

"How did you get it?" they clamoured. "What did it feel like?"

I frowned. I didn't want to confide in these girls on the new unit, I barely knew them. They'd no idea about me and Dougie. I presumed the love-bites were from him, during the time I'd blacked out, before leaving the flat. But I had no memory at all of getting them, certainly not of wanting to have them. A chill ran through me. If I didn't remember this – what else did I not remember? I was pinning my hopes on Dougie being different than all the other men I'd met. What if he was just as bad? Or worse? I didn't want to be a victim. I could not allow myself to be like my mother. This just wasn't me. The other girls were impressed. A love bite, at our age, was a badge of honour, a status symbol.

"Wow, Hope, I'm so jealous. Wish I had a fella. Wish I had a love bite like that."

"Yeah," I smiled, uncertainly. "You're right. I'm lucky really."

"Is this why you got moved into the unit?" they asked. "Is it because of your boyfriend?"

"Something like that," I nodded.

I played along with the gossip but deep down, I felt uneasy. I had no idea what had happened in the flat to make me want to leave so abruptly. I couldn't remember why I'd gone to the phone box. I didn't recall the conversation with the operator or with the staff. One thing was certain; I must have been absolutely desperate to call the children's home for help. Confiding in the staff was a last resort, especially after the way they'd treated me by moving me to the new unit. I must have been frightened or in danger. Yet how could I possibly be in any danger, when I had Dougie to look after me? It didn't make sense. All night, the unanswered questions swirled, like smoke from one of Dougie's joints, around my head. But no matter how I tried, I just couldn't remember. There were tantalising snippets of the afternoon; twirling around dancing, grabbing onto the side of the door frame to stop myself falling, seeing the wavy walls come towards me in the empty bedroom. But I could not link them together. I could not stitch together the vital missing pieces. Wide awake in the early hours, I tried to delve into the recesses of my mind to dig out the information. But it was like reaching into a long tunnel with a short arm. Even with my fingertips outstretched, I just couldn't get to it. A couple of days later, Dougie called the phone in the new unit.

"How did you get through on this phone?" I asked.

"Never mind that. You vanished the other day," he said accusingly. "What did you do that for? You just pissed off. No explanation."

I hesitated. I'd hoped he might be able to answer that for me, might fill in those blanks. I ought to have confronted him, there and then. My consciousness was telling me very firmly to face this. Instead, I heard a slight edge in his voice, and I panicked. I didn't want to make him angry. I didn't want to lose him. We were getting married, after all. I was his princess. He loved me.

"Sorry Dougie," I said. "I just didn't feel well. I had to get some fresh air. Can I come round this weekend? Please?"

Even as I spoke, I was furious with myself. I didn't understand why my mouth was working without my brain's permission. All my senses told me I should be running a mile from this man. Yet here I was, pleading to be allowed to see him again. I was bewildered by my own duplicity; how could I let myself down like that? I had turned on myself, just as everyone else turned on me.

"Please?" I wheedled again.

Dougie let out a long sigh. I knew he was smoking. I pictured him, in the red phone box, leaning against the door, as though he owned it. There could be a queue outside, people waiting to make calls of their own, but Dougie would take his time and finish his cigarette. That was just how he was.

"I need to be able to rely on you," he said eventually. "You're my girl. I love you. I can't have you running away from me. Understand? You do as you're told."

"Yes, Yes," I babbled. "I'm sorry, it won't happen again. I promise."

"I'll be in the woods tomorrow night," he said. "See you then."

It was an order, not a question. But I tried not to think too deeply about it.

My eyes glistened with tears of relief as I hung up. I'd come so close to losing Dougie. I'd nearly ruined it, just as I ruined everything else in my life.

'Not so,' said a firm voice in my head. 'You ended up apologising for an incident which you know was Dougie's fault. You should never see him again. You're covered in love bites you can't explain. The man is a creep.'

'Dougie has been good to you,' said a louder voice. 'Those love bites are a small price to pay if they keep him happy. And anyway, how can it be Dougie's fault? You're the one who had the blackout. You're the one who drank too much. The responsibility is all yours.'

Oh, how I wished I could confide in Lara or one of the other girls from downstairs. I longed to see Issy. Or Marie. I needed their advice. I didn't trust the voices in my own head. I found it so hard to know what to do. That night, before bed, I stared in the bathroom mirror at the love bites. They were a mark of ownership. I belonged to him. They were a sign of how much Dougie loved me and how much he wanted the world to know it. Very deliberately, I closed my mind to my dissenting voice. Even if it was right, I didn't want to listen. And I knew I didn't have the courage to leave Dougie anyway.

20

THE NEXT night, Dougie and I hid in the woods and again, his kissing was so aggressive, I felt my head snapping back with the pressure. I didn't like it at all. But I couldn't tell him. I was afraid he might lose his temper, or worse, he might lose his interest in me. It was only kissing, after all. And I was prepared to put up with that if it meant we could get married. I had an alarming flashback to my mother, crying out in pain at the hands of a stranger in her own bed, and realised she had put up with much worse. I shook my head, hoping the image might physically fall out through my ears. I didn't want parallels with my mother's life. I didn't want to be like her. Yet these comparisons just kept popping up, like boils on the surface of my skin.

"So, do you remember what happened in the flat the other night?" Dougie asked, as he took a swig of his lager.

Wide-eyed, I shook my head.

"I felt a bit sick, um, I think I might have passed out," I confessed.

I hoped he wouldn't be annoyed that I couldn't hold my drink. But to my surprise, he laughed.

"I'll say this for you girl, you give good head," he said.

I rocked back, on my heels, as though someone had punched

me full in the face. I'd read plenty of magazines. I knew exactly what 'good head' meant. Yet why would Dougie possibly say such a thing? I'd never had oral sex, or any kind of sex, with anyone. Was he referring to my memory loss, in the flat? Was this what I had blanked out? Oral sex? The world seemed to tilt and tip me sideways, and I reached out to grab hold of a tree branch. I needed the reassurance of something solid. Dougie laughed again.

"You're a little cracker princess," he said. "See you next week."

And then, he was gone.

Stumbling back through the undergrowth, the voice I had silenced ripped back through my head, loud and clear.

'That's it, you must never see him again. Never. He's a weirdo. He's dangerous.'

"Yes," I shuddered. "That's right. He's a slimeball. It's over."

As I swung open the fire door, a feeling of relief trickled through me. At last, I had made my decision. I was done with Dougie. But back inside, the other voices, the wheedling, whining, persuasive voices, began spreading through my mind. They crept, like poison ivy, through the branches of my thoughts.

'Perhaps there's another meaning to his words. Possibly, you misheard or misunderstood. Maybe Dougie was joking, yes, that's it. He's always playing pranks, you know that. Anyway, how could you possibly have given Dougie oral sex, and not remembered it? That's crazy. You don't even know how to do oral sex!'

The voices clashed and collided as I went over what he had said, time after time after time. I wanted so much to talk to

Lara. I needed to say this out loud and hear another point of view. Ensnared in an emotional maelstrom of conflicting ideas and opinions, I just didn't know where to turn. When I'd first met Dougie, he was an injection of excitement and freedom into my life. It was like throwing myself off a drop slide; the adrenalin and exhilaration far outweighing the trepidation. Now, his presence felt like a toxin, seeping through my bones. How had it all gone so wrong?

Battling with my thoughts, I pulled my pencil case out of the drawer, and, like a robot, I took the compass and scratched down the inside of my thigh. I closed my eyes as blood trickled, warm and reassuring, down my leg. The relief was instantaneous. It was like an old friend, coming in, out of the darkness. My shoulders dropped and my whole body softened. With the compass in my hand, I found I didn't need to think about Dougie. I couldn't even really remember what he'd said. Not exactly. Probably, it was no big deal. I made another gouge into my skin and allowed myself to be carried off, on a rapturous wave of bliss.

'I love you, princess. You and me are going to be together.'

There was nobody else but Dougie for me. I wondered why I had ever doubted that. And if he didn't treat me nicely, well, maybe that was because it was all I deserved. It was my fault, not his. And if I was brutally honest with myself, my internal arguments were all largely speculative because there were no circumstances under which I would have refused to see Dougie.

Much as he appalled and frightened me at times, I could never have taken a stand against him. Each time I summoned the strength not to see him again, my body let me down and I found myself hurrying back to him, as though I was being operated on a remote control. He might just as well have had a huge magnet to reel me in like a little fish, gasping for air.

On the surface, I told myself I loved him, and I enjoyed spending time with him. I was his princess, and we were going to get married. Deeper, and murkier, was the tacit acceptance that I was not allowed to stop seeing him. I wanted to please him, but I was also afraid of angering him. Most of all, and most tragically of all, I was afraid of losing him. Because if not Dougie, then who did I have? Everyone I loved, or liked, was gradually stolen away from me, one by one, as the years passed.

I felt like one of the long grasses I sometimes picked in the woodland where I stripped away the stems, layer by layer, until there was nothing left. Until the grass was no more. Dougie was my everything because I loved him. And Dougie was my everything because I had nothing else. I was little more than a grassy stalk, stripped down, right to the core.

And so, the memory, or lack of it, of what had taken place inside the flat was gradually pushed into the dusty corners of my consciousness. All vestigial flickers of doubt which remained were quickly swatted away like wasps. By the time Dougie called the communal phone, to summon me once again, I was beginning to doubt the assault had ever happened in the first place.

The following Friday, I escaped out of the home and made my way to the station without a problem. Perversely, I was disappointed it was so easy. Why was nobody checking on me? Why did nobody care I was running away, yet again? They had all given up on me and written me off. Even my own name felt like a cruel play on words.

She's just like her mother, isn't she? Hope, the no-Hoper. Hope the Hopeless.

Dougie met me at Waterloo, and we went straight to the flat. Trev and Tammy turned up soon after, with a carrier bag full of booze. There was a rip in the carrier bag, so Tammy had to hold it underneath, to stop the cans falling out through the hole. For some reason, the sight of Tammy juggling the cans, with one hand over the rip, really upset me. We didn't even have a decent carrier bag and it seemed to speak of everything which was wrong with my life.

"Here," she said, plonking the bag onto the table and handing me a drink. "You alright? You look a bit peaky."

I shrugged and took a sip. I knew I ought to pace myself, after last time. I didn't want to irritate Dougie. I worried he might lose patience with me if I blacked out again. But I had to drink. I had to escape myself, somehow. Dougie rolled a joint and produced a pack of cards.

"Thought we might play a game this afternoon," he winked, and I gave him a brittle smile.

"Yeah, I'm up for it," I replied, with as much false enthusiasm as I could manage.

As we opened more drinks, there was a banging on the front door. Dougie clicked his tongue in annoyance as he went to answer. Tiffany appeared in the living room and threw herself down on the sofa, as if it was her home. Was it still her home? I didn't really know. Did she really believe she and Dougie were still together? Did I believe it? The boundaries were increasingly greyed and blurry. Dougie was married to Tiffany. Yet he was going to marry me. I didn't like the way that sounded, and so I elbowed the thought right out of my head. Dougie was still at the front door, arguing with a man, and I heard him shout:

"Don't care who you are, mate. Way I live my life is my business. Now piss off."

The door slammed and he reappeared, with a strained sort of smile.

"What did you have to bring your mouthy cousin round for?" he asked Tiffany. "If you've got a problem with me, tell me yourself, you don't need to hide behind him. You little snitch."

Dougie turned his back on Tiffany and carried on chatting and laughing with Trev. But there was tension in the room. I could feel Tiffany's eyes boring through the side of my head. She had taken off her coat, and she was resting her hands on her bump, as if to convey a message to Dougie. Perhaps to me, too.

"Tell you what, we'll go in the other room," Dougie said, picking up his drink, his bag of weed, and his pack of cards. "Leave you here, Tiff, on your own, eh?"

Me, Tammy and Trev all followed him into the second, empty, room and sat on the floor. Dougie slid the bolt across, before he sat down. It should have struck me as ominously incongruous that, although there was no furniture, not even a carpet, he had a lock on the door. But I was just pleased to be away from Tiffany and those eyes burning right through me. Moments later, we heard her banging on the other side of the door, demanding to be let in.

"Go away," Dougie yelled. "We're busy in here."

"Right, let's play," he continued, dealing the cards. "Who wants to play poker? Strip poker obviously, girls."

I searched his face for signs he was joking. He was not. Despite the cannabis shaving the edge off my anxiety, a panicky sensation rushed through me like a speeding car.

"What, like take our clothes off?" I asked. "That kind of strip-poker?"

"Yeah, dickhead," Dougie nodded. "What else would it mean?"

There was a hard glint in his eye. A metallic tone to his voice. And in that moment, the penny dropped. And the sound, as it hit the floor of my consciousness, rang out in my head. I knew, even then, the reverberations would never be silenced. With sickening clarity, I knew exactly what Dougie had in mind, and I didn't want it at all. This was no fairytale. It was not a fantasy. My daydream of us holding hands and exchanging kisses until we were married was laughably, absurdly, punishably, childish. I realised it now. But I realised it all too late. It was as though I'd aged 20 years in that one instant. Flashing before my eyes was the white backside, pumping up and down, on top of my mother, in my parents' bed. I heard the punter groan, and I remembered the way he had glared at me, over his shoulder.

"You want some, you little whore?"

I thought of the two brothers who pinched her hard on the chest and made her cry. And I remembered Albert, leaning over me in bed, as he pressed a cold, hard, treacherous coin into my small and grateful palm. As a little girl, I'd prided myself on my ability to weigh up our male visitors: Punter, or not? It was like a sick quiz show that I played in the privacy of my own brain. With Dougie, I'd taken my eye off the ball. I had melted, I had surrendered, I had allowed myself to dream. Because Dougie, in fact, was simply the next one along the conveyor belt. I saw him now for what he was: Punter.

"I don't want to play," I stammered. "I don't want to play strip poker."

141

"Doesn't matter what you want," Dougie replied, with an easy grin, as if my protest was of no consequence, which of course it wasn't. "Here, you have another go on this joint. That will shut you up."

The game started and my heart stuttered when I was dealt the lowest hand.

"Take off your jumper!" Dougie said gleefully.

I was wearing my favourite gypsy top underneath, the one which sat a little off the shoulder. Normally, I'd be all too pleased to show it off. Today, I felt oddly exposed and vulnerable.

"Nice," Dougie smiled, twanging my bra strap.

Tammy lost the next round. I lost the one after that. It didn't take me long to work out that Dougie was cheating. It wasn't a game at all. It was just a situation where we took our clothes off in front of leering men. By the time I was sitting in my bra and pants, Dougie had only lost a sock. Tammy was in her underwear too, trembling. She and I exchanged flickering glances of helpless fear. Like me, she hadn't said a word since the game started. There was no way out, for either of us. Every now and again, Tiffany would bang on the bedroom door and demand to come in, and Dougie would scoff and laugh in reply.

"Not long to go now, Hope," he smiled, with an approving glance at my underwear. I nodded weakly.

I was dreading taking off my underwear. But I didn't want to annoy Dougie either, especially not with Tiffany hammering on the other side of the door. She was a ready-made replacement for me, should I step out of line. Much as I loathed Dougie, in that moment, I did not want to lose him. I was stuck. Like a little ladybug, with my wings caught in a net, I was trapped.

"Here," Dougie said, and he handed me another can of lager.

I took it and had a sudden recollection of my mother accepting a glass of whisky from one of her punters, in the kitchen. Slowly, inevitably, my worst nightmare was becoming a reality, and I was turning into my mother. I was turning into everything I had always vowed I would not. I felt as though someone was shovelling sand into my mouth, blocking my windpipe, filling my lungs. I snatched at a breath not knowing when, or if, the next one would come.

"Smile," Dougie rapped, as he shuffled the pack. "Your face won't crack."

He dealt another round of cards, and I experienced a dull thud of acceptance when he announced I had the losing hand. Yet again, I was the loser. The poker game was a metaphor, it seemed, for my whole life. Lose, lose, lose. I removed my bra and huddled, with my knees hunched up to my chest, quivering in fear. I thought again of the ladybug and the way it had saved me, inside the dirty flat with the dirty man and the dirty film. Maybe I could do it again; perhaps I could become a little ladybug, and close my wings down around me, until the danger had passed. As I squeezed my eyes tight, there was a terrific banging on the door, and a man yelled:

"I know what you're up to. Open this door, you filthy git. Now!"

I recognised the angry voice because it belonged to Tiffany's cousin from earlier on. I could hear her yelling and banging too. There was a moment's pause and some muffled discussion before a loud crack made me jump. Tammy let out a small squeal of alarm.

"I've got an axe!" he yelled. "I'm coming in!"

Dougie stiffened.

"Let him try," he muttered. "As if. Fucking idiot. As if."

Each blow on the door was followed by a splintering sound. Once or twice, the door shook a little and the frame around it shivered as if it, too, was beginning to fear the worst. We all stared, fixated, waiting for Tiffany and her crazed cousin to come crashing in. After one loud thwack, the axe blade came poking through our side of the door, glinting as it caught the light. I was transfixed, as though I was watching a real-life horror film. Dougie nodded at the blade and smirked.

"Come on in," he said, spreading his arms wide. "Join in the fun!"

I didn't want Tiffany's angry cousin to axe his way in. Was he intending to axe his way through us too? I had no idea whether he was here to save us or attack us. And I was unsure too, whether I wanted to be saved. I didn't want to take off all my clothes for Dougie. But neither did I want to be taken away from him. As I wrestled with the polarity of feelings, there was more commotion outside, and a firm, authoritarian, male voice said:

"Open this door. This is the police."

Again, my thoughts swirled in a soup of uncertainty. This was my way out, my escape route. But did I want it? If the police came in, it would surely be the end of Dougie and me. I could not bear to even contemplate that. Another part of my life was ending. Another relationship was breaking. I was the common theme, running through all this tragedy, destruction, and heartache. This was my fault, just like everything else. Dougie got to his feet and welcomed the police into the bedroom as though he was doing them a favour. He was unruffled, unperturbed, even vaguely off-hand.

"You'd best cover yourself up," he told me, in a slightly mystified voice that suggested I'd been undressing for no good reason.

The humiliation I felt, huddled up on bare floorboards, wearing nothing but a pair of knickers, went way deeper than my lack of clothing.

"How old are you girls?" asked one of the officers. "Names? Addresses?"

As soon as I mentioned the children's home, the officer sighed wearily, as though I was a recurring inconvenience. I felt like a cold sore or a verruca. A persistent, annoying, time-wasting problem, to be avoided, if at all possible.

"Right, let's get you two to the station," he said.

Dougie and Trev sidled into the living room and didn't even say goodbye as we were taken out onto the landing. I was still trying to tie my laces and button up my jeans, as we waited for the lift. In the police car, a second officer asked me:

"So did the man with the axe touch you at all? Any injuries? Did he come near you with it at all? Threaten you?"

Numbly, I shook my head. I could not believe he saw the violence as the main issue. His only focus was the axe. My only focus was the shame and the pain. It felt so much worse, so much more wounding, than any damage Tiffany's cousin might have done with his axe.

"He didn't come anywhere near us with the axe," I mumbled.

The children's home staff came to collect me. There was no reference to me being found almost naked. No mention of why or how I was in a flat with two men, and bags of booze and drugs. Once it was established that I had no injuries from the axe, the police rapidly lost interest.

"You've really let yourself down, running away again," my residential worker told me crossly. "You're wasting everyone's time. Why can't you just do as you're told?"

And then came the killer blow.

"You know, Hope, you need to be careful. You'll end up like your mother if you carry on like this."

The words were like an axe blade, slicing through the back of my head.

21

BACK AT the children's home, curled up on my bed, my di-
lemmas clouded my brain like a thick curtain of London smog.
Instinctively, I knew what Dougie had done was wrong. The
strip poker game had exposed him as the monster my sensible
voice had warned me against.

'Told you so,' said the voice. 'What do you think would have
happened if that bloke hadn't turned up with the axe? He'd
have made you strip naked, and then what?'

I quivered. I'd come so close, so petrifying close, to disaster.
Yet, like the smog, my quandary was blurred and hazy, with
areas of grey.

'Dougie loves you,' said the louder, brasher, voice. 'He told
you so himself, lots of times. He wants to marry you. He wants
to be with you. He shows you more attention than anyone else
you know, and let's face it Hope,' and here, the voice sniggered,
'You are not in a position to be picky.'

It was a low blow, but it was true, I conceded sadly. I'd gladly
snatch at any kind of attention, good or bad, any shape, any
size. Anything at all. It occurred to me Dougie might even have
been arrested; the flat was filled with drugs. We were under-age
drinkers. I did not think for a moment he'd be in trouble for

locking an almost naked child in an empty bedroom. I blamed myself for that; not him. But a few days after the axe-attack, I was called to the communal phone, and I knew it had to be Dougie.

"Listen, don't worry about a thing," he said brightly when I picked up the receiver. "I can sort it all out. Nothing's gonna stop us being together. Nothing."

I was wrong-footed. He didn't mention anything about the strip poker, or Tiffany's cousin, or even the police.

"I'll sort it," he reassured me again. "You know that. I'll be in touch soon. I love you, princess."

And then, he was gone. I was perplexed. It was as though the incident at the flat had never happened. He didn't refer to it in any way. If anything, he was presenting himself as the solution and not the problem. Again, I wished I could talk to Lara, or any one of my mates from downstairs. I felt as though I was going mad. How could something so serious happen, like a stranger axing his way in through the door, and the police finding me almost naked, and yet Dougie not feel it was worthy of a casual reference? It was baffling. Unsettling. Had I imagined the whole episode?

I even considered telling a staff member, but I was too worried about the consequences. It wasn't as though I could confide in Callum or Issy, not anymore. I didn't know the staff in the new unit and there was nobody I could trust. And even though I was miserable here, I also knew it could get much worse. Telling the staff about Dougie would be like unravelling the biggest ball of wool and the whole story would have to come out. I'd find myself back in a secure unit, with a padded cell and a hatch in the door. I might even find myself in one of those dodgy children's homes where Jimmy Savile visited every week to take his pick. Careful what you wish for. And so, I was stuck on my own with my problems, whizzing round and round my head on a fast spin cycle, until I couldn't make sense of anything.

Perhaps, the brash voice told me, I had got it all wrong. Possibly, I had misremembered, or misread the situation, just as I had with Dougie's comment about 'giving good head'. Because of my own past, I had mistaken a fun game for something more sinister.

'You should be disgusted with yourself,' said the voice. 'You're adding a sexual element into a perfectly innocent situation. It was just a game of cards with a bit of a twist. That's all.'

Maybe that was it, then. It wasn't Dougie's fault. It was mine. He was the adult, after all. He seemed to have a grasp of things and he was confident he could look after me. It would be best to try to wipe the memories of the strip poker game from my mind and put my trust in him. Anyway, what other choice did I have? And so, as my thoughts turned and twisted, I found myself itching to see him again, desperate for his call, keen to go back for more. I could not explain it to myself. I don't understand it even now, as an adult. But I was being groomed and exploited and coerced, just as if he'd laced my drinks with a potion or put me under a curse. He wielded an influence and a power over me that, as a child, I was both repelled by and drawn to.

Looking back, I feel strongly that the move to the new unit, isolated and away from everyone I trusted, helped push me further into Dougie's lair. I had nobody else in my life and I felt angry, betrayed and rejected. Dougie seemed like the answer. Yet I wasn't really sure of the question.

Those days after his phone call seemed to drag. I couldn't

think of anything else. Having vowed to stay away from him, I now began to panic that maybe I wouldn't hear from him. The thought of a world without Dougie was at once appealing and petrifying.

In this new unit, I had nothing else to do except think of him. I'd given up on my Duke Of Edinburgh award. I'd stopped playing the drums. I went to the occasional history lesson but that was only because the teacher came to my room and pleaded with me to carry on. I even gave up my Saturday job, in the bakery, which I had loved.

"We'll really be sorry to see you go, Hope," my boss said. In truth, I was sorry to leave.

My books gathered dust as I stopped reading. For me, that was like stopping breathing. But I was taking a stand, in my own, stubborn way, punishing myself, retreating into myself, in protest at the way I was being treated. Maybe, deep down, I hoped to provoke a reaction from the staff, and I wanted someone to grab me by the shoulders and march me back to my job, back to my drum lessons, back to my old life.

Yet this new unit was all about independence and self-motivation, and so the staff didn't intervene or question my choices at all. I don't think they even noticed I'd given up everything I enjoyed. Instead, I was left to flounder and to slowly sink. Catastrophically, the only activity I didn't give up was self-harming. Dragging the compass along my flesh was the only form of release I could find. And even then, like a petrol haze, it shimmered and vanished within seconds. That Friday, after lunch, Dougie called again.

"I want to see you," he said softly. "I've missed you princess. I need to see you. Today."

A blush crept up my neck as I whispered down the phone, my hand cupped over the receiver.

"Me too," I said quietly. "But there's no way I can get away. I think the staff will be watching the train station this afternoon. I'm in big trouble after, well, after the fuss at the flat…"

My voice trailed off. I felt guilty for even bringing it up, as though it was nothing to do with Dougie. As though I was the one who had caused the scene. He just laughed.

"I've got a better idea than that," he replied. "I told you I'd sort it, and I have. Just you wait and see. You come outside, about 7pm. Back entrance. I'll be waiting."

"You're coming here?" I said, my voice rising with a mixture of anticipation and alarm. "Tonight?"

"Yeah, I'm coming there, and I'm coming for you," he said. "Don't let me down."

I could tell from his voice how much he'd missed me. When he hung up, I strolled down the corridor, back to my room, holding my secret inside of me, like a precious jewel. Dougie was coming to the children's home. Especially for me. Only for me. Looking back, I despair at how easily I was talked around, how little it took to blackmail me and to win my trust. I wish I'd put up more of a fight, made myself more of a challenge. More than anything, I wish I'd walked away. Even now, a small part of me still blames myself.

I was so focused on meeting Dougie; I couldn't concentrate on my afternoon lessons. I barely ate any dinner. I just wanted to get away.

"You okay, Hope?" asked one of the staff. "You're very quiet."

"Yeah, I think I'm coming down with something," I said. "Might go up and have an early night."

I walked slowly out of the dining room, one hand clutching at my imaginary stomach pain. The moment I got around the corner, out of sight, I broke into a run, laughing to myself as I shot down the corridor and out into the gardens. Waiting in the woods, with Dougie, were Trev and Tammy.

"Hiya," I smiled. "Didn't realise you were coming."

I was so glad to see Tammy. And her being here was further proof that I'd got it all wrong, about the strip-poker. She was happy, after all, to come back for more. So I should be too.

"We've got a surprise for you girls," Dougie said, swapping his carrier bag onto his other arm so he could take my hand. I could hear bottles and cans clinking in the bag and I smiled to myself. This was shaping up to be a good night.

"What is it?" I asked.

"Follow me," he winked. "You'll soon see."

22

AT THE other side of the woods, not far from the children's home, there was a derelict house. It was on the roadside but hidden by overgrown bushes and weeds, and I'd never taken too much notice of it until now. Dougie pushed open the rusty gate and marched up the path with his usual swagger, as though he owned the place. There was a long-dead bird in the garden, crawling with maggots. The head, half-eaten, was missing an eye. It felt like a warning, and I shuddered.

"Come on," Dougie said impatiently, as I hung back.

'Run. Run now,' shouted the dissenting voice. It sounded so far away, and yet it was at screaming pitch. 'Run!'

My mind, truly, wanted to run. But my legs just kept on following Dougie up the path. I was somehow under his control, unable to stand up to him. I could not explain it and nor could I fight it.

"This is ours, for tonight anyway," he said grandly, kicking open the front door.

It wasn't locked. It wasn't even properly closed. And inside, the hallway was dark and smelled of damp. There was a windowpane missing and a few loose floorboards, by the doorway.

"This is so spooky," said Tammy, with a little shiver.

I nodded. My enthusiasm was quickly draining, like dirty water out of a sink. I thought of all the fairytales I'd ever read, where the characters stumbled across a remote house in the woods, Little Red Riding Hood, Hansel and Gretel, Goldilocks. It never ended well. Nothing good ever came of going into houses like this.

"Come on," Dougie said again, leading the way upstairs.

Reluctantly, I followed, up onto a landing, and into a large room. Like the rest of the house, it was empty, with bare boards and no curtains. I felt horribly uncomfortable. The atmosphere was charged, as if we were waiting for a storm. And yet outside, it was a mild evening.

Dougie produced cans and we started drinking. But my heart just wasn't in it. The lager was warm and left a sour taste in my mouth. Tammy was very quiet too, though Dougie and Trev didn't seem to notice. As it grew darker outside, Dougie began kissing me, pushing me backwards, so I was lying down on the floorboards, with him on top of me. He didn't speak and neither did I. In years to come, I would hate myself for not fighting back, or at least speaking out. My passivity, my quiet and pitiful acceptance of my fate, would form the bedrock of my shame throughout the rest of my life. I blamed myself, for this, as for everything else. Dougie didn't force me, and he didn't threaten me. He didn't have to. I just lay there obediently and let it happen because I did not know what else to do. I thought, by saying nothing, I could have it all over and done with, as quickly as possible. And in many ways, it felt inevitable. What were my options? I could try to fight back and have Dougie smack me in the face to make me compliant. How would that help? Any protest would have been useless.

My mind's eye flickered with snapshot memories; the piss-soaked bed of my childhood, watching strangers having sex with my mother; taking money from the posh punter with the briefcase; staggering to the phone box with a love bite on my neck; telling myself I'd misheard when Dougie told me: 'You give good head'; convincing myself I'd misunderstood a game of strip poker. The final snapshot, more of a brutal realisation, was me, alone and sobbing in a bare room; groomed, used and ruined by a paedophile. They were all stages along the way. And this was the end game. A small whimper escaped my lips, and I bit back, anxious not to make a sound and get myself into trouble or delay proceedings. I was aware the same thing was happening to Tammy, just next to me. I reached out, stretching my fingers, hoping to find her hand. I sensed I could almost touch her. Nearly. But not quite. Afterwards, I heard her crying, softly, in the darkness. Dougie fell asleep, and then Trev. I lay awake, till dawn, relieved, at least that it was done. In the back of my mind, though I'd never considered it, I'd probably always known I could not escape this.

'Why do adults have sex?' I wondered.

Why put themselves through such a painful, horrible, ordeal? I couldn't work it out. The next morning, I didn't speak. I grabbed my jeans and my shoes, and we walked out, into the early sunshine, as though nothing had happened. The blue skies felt like a final twist of the knife, as though the weather was mocking my trauma. There was something clean and fresh about the air, first thing in the morning, and it jarred horribly.

Nobody cares about you, Hope. The sun's out, everyone's happy. Happy that you've been raped.

I noticed a small sliver of slime in the corner of Dougie's

eye, and it disgusted me. The bile rose in my throat, and I bent double, on the pavement, gulping in fresh air. Dougie didn't seem to notice my distress. He didn't comment. He didn't care. I walked alone back to the children's home and the others went to the train station. The duty night manager was about to clock off and she bumped into me in the entrance hall.

"You're right at the bottom of the status chart, Hope," she snapped. "We know you were out all night. You've lost everything. No late nights. No treats. No takeaways. No pocket money."

Well, she was right about one thing. I had lost everything. It resonated loudly to be at the bottom of the status chart too because it was exactly where I belonged. I had zero status. I was worth nothing. I was so sore down below, I felt sure I was injured in some way. It hurt to walk, it hurt even more to sit down. But I couldn't confide in anyone, without admitting what I'd been doing. I was so ashamed of myself for having sex. And sex with someone else's husband, too. I couldn't begin to confess such an atrocity to the staff. I knew how they'd judge me because it was just how I judged myself.

You are a little whore. You are a little slag. You are a little slut.

23

DOUGIE CALLED me three days later.

"Hey princess," he said. "How about it, tonight? I can get you out of there. Leave it to me. Just meet me, usual place, 7ish."

I made a funny sound, a sob strangling in my throat, and Dougie's tone sharpened.

"Make sure you're there. Don't piss me about. Don't start. Fucking hell, first Tiffany, now you."

Just the mention of her name was enough to snap me back into line.

"I won't," I promised. "I'll be there."

"Good girl," he replied, softer now. "Love you, princess."

And that was all I needed. That was how easily I was won over. I replaced the receiver with my heart singing. He loves me, he loves me, he loves me. Dougie was my hero, my saviour, my salvation. Besides, I was at the bottom of the status chart, in the children's home and in life. I was worth nothing, so I also had nothing left to lose.

For much of my adult life, my pain has focused not on the rape itself, which I would not even recognise as such for many years to come. My real and lasting trauma lies in the detail; my frustration, my fury, at how effortlessly Dougie groomed me.

He never once bought me a present. He didn't have to. Would I have felt any better if he'd won me round with chocolates and designer clothes? Probably not. He never threatened me, or hit me, or coerced me. I feel so angry at my 15-year-old self for not putting up any resistance. Would I have coped better if he'd punched me before the rape? Probably not. I never tried to avoid meeting Dougie and sometimes I couldn't wait to see him.

Even after that first rape, I went back, willingly, for more. I don't know why. If I'd run from him, hidden away, tried to escape, would I feel proud of myself? Probably not. But it is these details, each as painful as a slither of glass stabbing right through my heart, which haunt me. This is the true cost of child grooming and child sexual exploitation. It is like dry rot, spreading through your entire mind and body, ruining everything past, present and future. The act of rape itself, whilst unspeakably horrific, is only one part of an appalling and putrid process.

As I walked down the corridor, after Dougie's call, I felt a stinging sensation down below. The initial soreness had worsened, and now it burned every time I used the toilet. I was too frightened to tell the staff in case they could somehow link it to me having sex. I was so scared of anyone finding out. But that urine infection was the first of many. Even now, I am plagued by cystitis and urinary tract infections, and I can trace them back to the violation in the derelict house. The abuse by Dougie was like a boulder, dropped into the waters of a still pond, and the ripples and ramifications continue to unsettle and upset me. Cystitis is by no means the worst problem he left me with. But it is a permanent reminder, and it is yet another scar.

"Let's go back to that place," Dougie said, when we met up that evening.

As usual with him, it was a decision, not a suggestion, and I dragged along behind, my limbs as heavy as concrete, the stinging pain intensifying with every step I took. Tammy and Trev were there too, but he had his arm around her waist, and she barely looked up. I felt like a little lamb, trotting into the slaughterhouse, the path to the derelict house. On the path, I saw the poor bird again, out of the corner of my eye, and I retched.

"Get inside," Dougie hissed. "Before someone sees you."

He pulled me in through the door and kicked it shut.

"Don't know why you're playing hard to get. You know you want it," he laughed as he clattered up the staircase, two steps at a time.

In many ways, that second time was worse, because I knew what was coming. I was already in pain, and now it was going to hurt so much more. I drank as much lager and smoked as much weed as I could, hoping to blot it out. Yet when the moment came, I was stone-cold sober. Every nerve in my body was alert and oozing dread. Again, I made no objection, I didn't struggle in any way, I didn't try to run away. I neither participated nor protested. I was completely passive. I accepted this was all I was good for. This was all I deserved.

This time, I managed to reach out to Tammy, and we hooked fingers. As I felt the reassurance of her skin on mine, there was a moment of absolute calm, for even in the middle of a hurricane, there is a millisecond of peace whilst the wind catches its breath. And then, it started again. Dougie rasped and grunted like a wild boar, an acrid smell of sweat and bodily fluids stinging my nose and eyes. And then, the grunting became a roaring in my ears, as I was ripped into two by a surge of unbearable pain.

"Won't be long till we're together all the time," Dougie told me, as he rolled over, ready to sleep. "What d'ya think of that, princess? We can do it every night."

My throat was too tight for words and instead, I nodded, through the darkness. My inside voice, louder now, was raging at me for not making my feelings clear. Why did I not stand up and leave the house, there and then? Why didn't I tell him he was a paedophile and a bully and a rapist? The gut-wrenching truth was, I was grateful for his words. His assurances washed over me, like balm. Even after the monstrous savagery of the rapes, I clung to the belief that one day, Dougie would want me as his wife. The sadness, when I think of this now, is unbearable.

Early the following morning, the welcoming party back at the children's home was more like a lynch mob. It appeared all the senior staff members were there, despite it not even being breakfast time yet. Sally, the big boss, took the lead. She was in charge of both units. She was responsible for double the misery, double the pain.

"We know exactly where you've been," she said, her voice ringing out in triumph. "You were seen, last night, going into the derelict house up the road. We've had phone calls. From neighbours. We know, Hope, we know."

I stared at her, physically crushed by her words, as though I was, again, a small ladybug and I was under her heel. If they knew where I was, why had nobody come to rescue me? Why had they just left me there, all night? How was it that I was considered too vulnerable to go to the shop on my own, yet it was okay to leave me in a derelict house overnight? The shock was not that they knew where I had been, but rather that they had done nothing about it.

"Oh yes," Sally said, with the air of someone who is about to deliver a marvellous punchline. "And we know who you were with."

She paused, unsmiling, for dramatic effect, to gauge my reaction. But my face was blank. I felt desolate beyond words. I was sinking.

"Tiffany called here last night," she continued. "She told us you've been having an affair with her husband. You're having an affair with your friend's husband. Your pregnant friend's husband. You seduced a married man. A family man. That's disgusting, Hope, do you understand?"

I felt myself sinking further, through the tiled floor, into the ground. The earth piled onto my head, clods of mud in my ears and my mouth. I just wanted it to be over.

"Hope!" she snapped. "You should be ashamed of yourself. You are a disgrace."

And oh yes, I was ashamed. It was a shame I carried like a tumour, a shame which dragged, like a brace on my leg, like a clamp on my heart. Who would want me after what I had done? I was a homewrecker. I was a slut, a whore, a slag. I was infected. I was my mother.

Nobody could condemn me as harshly as I condemned myself.

24

IN THE car, the next morning, there was a stony silence. It was a measure of the gravity of my crimes that Sally herself was taking me to the hospital. Her fury had been replaced by thinly veiled disgust and a sense of disappointment, though not unexpected, that I had let everyone down so badly.

"You need to see a sexual health nurse," she told me, as we pulled up outside the hospital. "Let's hope, for your sake, you're in the clear."

I did, at least, get anti-biotics for my UTI, but the embarrassment crippled me. With her face set, and her eyes staring stonily ahead, Sally marched me through the hospital corridors. I felt I was being paraded, like a fallen woman, as a warning to others. They might just as well have stoned me to death. And yet, of course, I was not a woman. I was a child. It was a fact which nobody, to my knowledge, raised at all, so much so I had forgotten it myself. I was not offered support or therapy or help of any kind, beyond a physical swab.

It had to be my fault, I told myself, it had to be. I had destroyed Tiffany's marriage and I had ruined my own reputation. My future lay in tatters. I felt lower than ever before. Back at the unit, I lay on the floor in my room, drained of the strength to even climb into bed. One of the staff popped her head around the door, and said:

"Do you want to talk about it, Hope?"

There was kindness in her voice, and I shuffled into a sitting position.

"You know, you really shouldn't let a bloke upset you like this," she said, as she perched on the end of my bed. "This is what men are like, pet. They use you for sex and then they blank you. You need to steer clear."

She meant well, but her words just reinforced in me the belief that I had brought all of this on myself.

"Look, I have to get back to work but I'll come and check on you later on," she said. "Try and snap out of it. Don't let him win."

Little did she know, he had won long ago. Alone again in my room, and desperate for release, I searched in my bedside drawer for a compass. Anything sharp. Anything would do. Instead, I came across a packet of painkillers. I couldn't remember ever buying them. Without following my thought process to the end, I popped the tablets out of the blister pack and swallowed as many as I could. As the powdery formula hit the back of my throat, I began dry retching, but I held them down.

Slowly, my self-loathing eased into feelings of acceptance and redemption. This was the best way for me to leave. This was the best way, the only way, for me to say sorry. I was, after all, a little slut, a little whore, a little slag. The dark thoughts spread like spilled ink through the layers of my consciousness. I lay down on the bed and waited. But as the minutes ticked by, I began to doubt myself. Faint glimmers of hope, like embers, glowed in my soul. I didn't want to die. I didn't want this. I was not a quitter. I had a fleeting image of my parents, sitting at our old formica table, swigging from chipped cups filled with whisky. I did not miss them but, at that moment, I missed the idea of them. I wanted a mum and dad.

The seeds of doubt quickly bloomed into full-blown panic, and I flew off the bed and rushed to the room next door, screaming for help. The girls clustered around and yelled for the staff. It was high but short-lived drama for them, I was not the first to cry for help and I would not be the last. I was bundled into a car and driven back to hospital, where I was made to drink a thick, black sludge. After a night on the ward, vomiting violently, I was discharged back to the children's home. I was not expecting sympathy or support and I was not disappointed. The staff seemed even more annoyed with me than before.

"It's attention-seeking, plain and simple," Sally said. "It can't continue. We can't have you here any longer Hope. I'm sorry, but you've brought this on yourself."

At first, I presumed I was being returned to a secure unit and I froze in fear. But she said:

"We're looking for a foster home for you."

This was, she explained, specialist foster care, targeted at particularly challenging kids, who were no longer considered suitable for a normal family. This was not Debs and Daz and the pink bedroom. It was not the stuff of dreams. Yet, I reminded myself, it was still a foster family. It was still a chance. This was, after all, what I had wanted so desperately and for so long. I was torn between the excitement of getting a home of my own at last, and the sadness at being moved on, yet again. I didn't want to leave my friends behind. I didn't want to leave Callum and Issy and the staff from downstairs. At least here, I knew they were nearby, even if I couldn't see them. I felt rejected and dumped. Most of all, I felt angry with myself. Nobody wanted me, and it was no surprise. These feelings were familiar but that did not mean they got any easier.

* * * *

Needless to say, I was grounded indefinitely, whilst the staff tried to find me a suitable foster home. They had clamped down on personal phone calls, vetting everyone who came through the system. I still firmly believed Dougie would find a way round it; he always did. I spent half my time dreading his call and the other half longing for it. But there was nothing. He seemed to just vanish off the face of the earth. Each day seemed to bring with it a new mishmash of emotions. I was relieved, certainly. But I missed him too; I missed everything he had stood for, the promises he had made, the hope he had offered. Even if it was false hope, it was all I had, and I'd been grateful for it.

There was an enduring sense of loss, a grief almost, for what I would never have. The 'what ifs' were like little knives, stabbing at my heart. The white wedding, the fairytale ball, the happy marriage; it all disappeared in a puff of smoke, just like Cinderella's carriage at midnight. I was jealous too, driving myself mad imagining Dougie and Tiffany in the flat, together. Was that why he hadn't contacted me? Was he back with her? I'd hoped he would, at least, be devastated at losing me. Perhaps, like everyone else, he was glad to get rid of me.

As an adult I can see Dougie was doubtless rattled when he discovered Tiffany had spilled the secrets of his affair with the staff at the children's home. He was thoughtless, but not completely stupid, and would have realised he was risking trouble by trying to contact me again. Now his identity was out, he simply dropped me like a brick.

Apart from monitoring the calls, the staff did little to enforce my punishment. I continued running away, but after my move to foster care was confirmed, they seemed to lose interest in what I was doing. I dropped down yet another rung.

"If she wants to put herself in danger, let her," I overheard a social worker say.

They were past caring. It was a depressing anti-climax, and also a damning indictment, to arrive back after one, maybe two nights away, and find the staff had not even missed me. There was no speech, no punishment, no discipline. Nothing. Much as I dreaded their fury, their indifference destroyed me. I was officially beyond redemption.

My 16th birthday passed, and if I received any gifts, I certainly don't remember them. There was no party, no big celebration. I had really hoped for something with 16 on it; a memento such as a balloon, or a badge, or even a 16th birthday card. Sweet 16 was part of my fairytale, and though it was spooling away from me, I still grabbed, desperately, at strands. I longed for recognition that I was 16, I wanted to make it official. Perhaps I just needed validation that I was actually still breathing. Just days after my birthday, my social worker called and told me to pack my stuff.

"Your new foster home is ready, Hope," she said. "I'll pick you up tomorrow morning."

She didn't sound as upbeat as I might have expected. Perhaps it was bitter-sweet for her too, seeing me shunted on, yet again, like faulty goods. There was no emotional goodbye, no farewell party. I wasn't even allowed to go downstairs to see my friends and the old staff, one last time. Instead, I slunk out of the front door, like a fox in the night, under a cloud of someone else's shame. It confirmed my belief that all of this was my fault.

"Look after yourself, Hope," said my keyworker.

He was the only one who came outside, to wish me luck. My stuff had already been packed for me, into bin-bags. I didn't have a suitcase or even a vanity bag; everything I owned was chucked into plastic refuse sacks, each time I moved. Anything delicate was broken, anything valuable was lost. But I had reached the stage where I didn't really care. I disassociated myself from possessions and from people; in my experience, neither lasted very long.

I had learned to live without my parents, my siblings and my friends. And so living without a few photos or a teddy bear was not difficult. Even today, aged 49, I could walk out of my flat, and leave it all behind, without so much as a backward glance. And my experience was by no means unique. It was the same for every other kid in care too. Our belongings were carted from one home to the next, in black bin bags. Rubbish bags. The analogy could not have been clearer.

25

MY FIRST impression, as we turned into the street, was a good one. My new foster parents lived in an upmarket area and their semi-detached home, on a corner, looked like a nice, neat little house. Inside, I was introduced to a middle-aged couple called Marj and Brian. Marj offered me a pudgy hand and I shook it and smiled.

"I'm Hope," I said.

Despite my despair, I wanted this to work. I wanted so much to be happy here. I could feel all the good intentions, all the promises, rattling around inside my mouth, bursting to get out. But I kept them to myself. I didn't want to bombard my new foster parents. I was wary of talking too much.

Brian, I thought, looked very much like the TV character Worzel Gummidge. He had a long nose and a toothless grin. Unlike Worzel, he had a long, wiry beard and it struck me he might have old fishfingers and bits of rubbish hidden away in there, like Roald Dahl's Mr Twit. The house was not as nice as it looked from the outside; the furnishings were shabby and worn. In the living room was an old chocolate brown sofa with a raised pattern, in long lines, which reminded me of self-harming scars.

"I'll show you your bedroom in a minute," Marj said. "Then you can get settled in."

The social worker took that as her cue to leave and it was just me, Marj and Brian. I felt strangely homesick and out of my depth, as I lingered in the hallway. I did not even know which home I was pining after, or if it was possible to miss somewhere you'd never even been. But I felt so out of place.

"Can I please call Lara, my friend at the children's home?" I asked. "I promised I'd give her a quick ring, let her know I'd arrived safely."

Marj blew air out from her round cheeks.

"Well, we have rules about the phone, see," she said. "You have thirty minutes a week of phone time and not a single second more. Every time you make a call, I get a receipt, so I know exactly what you've been up to."

I had no idea whether this was true or not, or even if it was possible, but the premise seemed outrageous.

"Half an hour a week?" I asked. "How long do the other kids get? How long do your kids get?"

"Ah well," Marj replied. "My kids don't have a time limit because they don't abuse the telephone. The rule is only for you foster kids."

Something snapped and pinged within me. All my good intentions were sucked away, replaced by angry protests, which surged to the surface.

"That's so unfair," I complained. "I've only just arrived. How can you possibly know whether I'm going to abuse the phone?"

Marj put her hands on her ample hips.

"Thirty minutes per week," she said. "And not a second longer, mind."

Being in the care system was a curse. I might as well have had: 'Liar, thief, vandal' tattooed across my forehead. It seemed so unjust. I'd been tried, convicted and sentenced before I'd even arrived here, for crimes I hadn't yet committed. Bristling, I reminded myself, I'd only just walked into this house, and I needed to get off on a good start. This was a foster home, it was what I'd wanted for so many years, and I had to make an effort.

"Okay," I agreed, swallowing my resentment. "Are there any kitchen rules?"

"Yeah," Marj said. "You bet."

She waddled into the kitchen, which was at the back of the house. Immediately, I noticed there were two fridges side by side.

"Foster kids' cupboard this side," she said, pointing a fat finger. "Natural kids, the other side. That's your fridge on the left, don't you touch the one on the right."

"What's the difference?" I asked suspiciously.

"None of your bloody business, young lady," she rapped. "Their cupboard is locked. Their fridge is out of bounds. You stick to your own."

I looked her up and down, taking in her piggy eyes clouded with dislike, her rolls of fat spilling over the top of her skirt, and I said nothing. But at that moment, I declared silent battle. I would make it my bloody business, I vowed. This was supposed to be my new home yet already I felt ostracised, humiliated and unwelcome. I was being treated like an animal. Worse, even. But it was not in my nature to cry under my duvet and feel sorry for myself, neither would I give in and allow myself to be bullied. Like a wounded animal, I would bite back.

Upstairs, I was shown into a room with two single beds, which I would be sharing with a girl named Cara. In the second bedroom was a foster boy called Kev. The third bedroom was occupied by the two 'natural' children, both girls. The fourth belonged to Marj and Worzel Gummidge.

After Marj had gone downstairs, I perched on the end of the bed, clutching my black bin bag on my knee. My hands, wrapped tightly around the bag, didn't feel like mine. I found it hard to distinguish between myself and my luggage; I felt like just another bag, transported from one home to another, from one bedroom to another. Each move chipped away a little more at my self-esteem and my character, until I felt weakened and diluted. I could hardly remember who I was. It seemed to me I had more in common with an inanimate object like a bin-bag, rather than the girl I had once been.

I had been enrolled at a college in the next town, to study A-levels, and I had an appointment to meet my personal tutor that afternoon. I was looking forward to returning to education, in the real world. All of my lessons, except those wonderful design and technology sessions, had been taught inside the children's home. I couldn't wait to sit in an actual classroom with actual teachers. But my heart sank when I realised just how far away the college was. I checked the directions and worked out I'd have to walk through two fields and then along a road to get to the station, before taking a train to college.

"Could I please have a lift to the station?" I asked Marj.

She shook her head.

"Too busy," she replied. "You'll have to walk."

It was early evening by the time I got back to the foster home from college. As I rang the doorbell and waited, my limbs aching with exhaustion, I realised already this would never be my home. The other kids were back from school and college, and, after we were introduced, it turned out Kev had been in the same children's home as my brothers, when he was younger.

"They used to talk about you all the time," Kev smiled.

The revelation made my heart leap and fall, all at once. I loved to hear about my brothers, but his words brought into sharp focus just how much I missed them. It turned out I had a link with Cara too. She was pregnant, and expecting a baby with a boy who'd gone out with a girl I knew from a previous children's home. It was further proof that the care circle was a small one; kids in care relied upon each other or ruined each other; perhaps at the same time.

Kev, Cara and I were around the same age, and I could tell we were going to get on well. It cheered me up to think I'd at least have allies against Marj and Worzel. And the two natural children, little girls, younger than me, were adorable. Much as I resented their golden status, I knew it wasn't their fault, and I couldn't help warming to them.

"We saw you earlier, Hope," said the older one. "Our school is opposite the train station. Mummy pointed you out, coming out of the station, when she picked us up."

"Oh," I said heavily.

It was not surprising to learn Marj had made me walk all the way to the station, when she was driving the same route herself. But it stung just the same. I tried again.

"Please can I have a lift tomorrow?" I asked. "I know you're driving to the train station. I won't be any trouble."

Marj shook her head.

"I've told you this once," she said. "I'm not driving you about. I need to focus on my natural children. I don't have time for the likes of you."

So what did that make me? Unnatural? A freak of nature? Maybe she was right. For our evening meal, Marj served up nuggets and oven chips for Kev, Cara and me. I stared at my plate in dismay. I'd had enjoyed home-cooked, healthy food at the children's home. I wasn't used to junk. The portions were so small too. Oddly, now I was in a home environment, I was eating institution food. Marj's two little daughters had eaten separately with their parents, and I was beginning to see the pattern here: two fridges, two cupboards, two totally different menus.

"Are there no vegetables?" I asked.

Marj shot me a sharp look which was, I knew, designed to silence me. But that was my problem; I could not keep quiet, even when, especially when, I was under orders. Cara quietly pushed the anaemic looking chips around her plate and said nothing. Kev raised his eyebrow at me in silent warning. But I just couldn't help myself.

"Can I have vegetables please?" I asked. "Frozen peas maybe? An old carrot? Anything will do. I'll cook them myself."

Without even looking at me, Marj swooped down, snatched my plate, and tipped it into the bin.

"We don't like moaners," she spat. "If you don't like it, don't eat it, young lady."

I could feel my anger coming to the boil, bubbling right in the back of my throat. But I said nothing. After Marj had gone into the living room, I peeked inside the foster kids' cupboard, and it was empty. I opened the foster kids' fridge, but there was nothing but lard and milk in there.

"It's always empty," Kev told me. "If you're hungry, you're better off buying your own food, whilst you're at college. That's what I do."

I went to find the two little girls, to distract myself, and spent that first evening brushing their long hair and doing fancy French braids. As I listened to them chatting and comparing styles, I thought of my own two long-lost sisters, the babies Mum had given up for adoption before I was born. They were another missing piece of my puzzle. Someone else I had lost. That night, in bed, I couldn't sleep, despite being so tired. My stomach rumbled as my temper simmered.

"What's in the locked cupboard?" I whispered to Cara. "The one we're not allowed to open?"

I heard Cara shrug in the darkness.

"It's for their kids," she replied. "I've never seen inside it."

"Stuff that," I replied.

I waited until the house was quiet and then I crept downstairs and snapped the cupboard lock. It was pathetically easy to break, I only had to slide a knife down the side. I had even less respect for Marj and Worzel now. They deserved this. And when the cupboard door swung open, my eyes lit up. Stacked, in piles, were family packs of Gold chocolate bars. With a smothered giggle, I took the lot and tiptoed back upstairs. I didn't even bother closing the cupboard. I didn't care that they knew it was me. In fact, I wanted them to know. I thought of Marj's piggy eyes, and her stupid, cruel rules and I laughed softly to myself.

"Just wait until you see the kitchen tomorrow," I said under my breath, as I passed her bedroom door.

I tapped lightly on Kev's door and together with Cara, we devoured the lot.

"God, that was lovely," Cara whispered, flopping back on her bed. "I've never had so much chocolate in my life."

The fall-out, the following morning, was nuclear. But the more Marj shouted, the more I laughed.

"Just to be clear," she yelled. "You, young lady, must never open that cupboard again! You're a foster kid. Don't forget it!"

There was no chance of that. She even insisted on frog-marching me around the house, pointing out everything I was not allowed access to.

"You're not to go into my daughters' bedroom or into my bedroom," she shouted. "And don't you ever touch my Avon make-up. Ever. I mean it. You touch that, and you've had it, young lady."

I nodded as solemnly as I could but inside, I was already gleefully planning my next mission. The next morning, I had a couple of free periods at college. Marj left the house early to take her daughters to school, leaving Worzel at home. I made sure he was outside, in the backyard, before I hurried into her bedroom and settled myself at her dressing table mirror. I applied generous amounts of foundation, eyeshadow and eyeliner, before peering at myself in the mirror. With a quick swipe of lipstick, I was done.

"Lovely," I said out loud. "Thanks Marj!"

When Marj came home later, she stared accusingly at my face and said:

"Is that my best Avon foundation mousse you're wearing?"

"Absolutely not," I lied, holding back my laughter. "I wouldn't dream of it."

It was only as the days went by, and the mousse foundation depleted at a startling rate, that Marj finally was able to pin the blame on me. I had used quite a lot of her eye make-up too, even though I wasn't overly keen on her colour scheme.

"You are a thief!" she screeched. "Stay away from my Avon make-up. I mean it!"

For some reason, the angrier she got, the funnier I found it. Her face would quickly become purple, her eyes disappearing into her puff-pastry cheeks, and the overall effect was hilarious. Besides, I didn't take her seriously. The way I saw it, I was simply getting even. Marj and Worzel received a fostering allowance, higher than usual because of my well-documented 'challenging behaviours'. And none of it was being passed on to me. Pinching her make-up was a little victory for me. And it kept me going, it gave me something to cling onto. That mousse foundation wasn't just make-up. It was my oxygen. It was my lifeline.

Marj had a reward chart, on the wall in the kitchen, with a star for each child every time they behaved well. I was not, needless to say, on her chart. I didn't receive a single reward and neither did I want one. I watched her handing out chocolate biscuits or crappy stickers as treats, and I didn't allow a single muscle in my face to betray me. There was no way I could ever have given her the satisfaction of knowing how worthless she made me feel.

"Don't like biscuits anyway," I told her, as she handed one out to everyone except me.

Marj snarled at me in reply. It was hard being marginalised. But it would have been harder still for me to give up whatever shreds of pride I had left. The battle lines were drawn, that first day, when I was banned from using the phone, banned from the fridge, banned from the cupboard. Banned from being a person.

26

IN THE evenings, after college, I worked in a One-Stop shop. I had to use my wages to buy toiletries and food, and whatever was left over, I spent on cigarettes and wine. Marj refused to collect me from work, even though it was a two-mile walk home in the dark. And so it didn't take long for me to decide not to bother going home at all. I was not permitted to have my own door key, because I was not trustworthy, and sometimes when I got back, I'd find the house in darkness. I spent hours huddled in the porch, waiting for her to come home, and let me in. It made more sense to me to stay out as late as I could.

One night, I went out drinking, with some college mates, and after they went home, I just walked the streets. It was liberating, wandering around aimlessly, on my own. As much as I'd longed for a home environment, I also found the practicalities of living in a house very claustrophobic. I'd been in institutions for so long that a house seemed small and confining to me.

I felt suffocated, by the small rooms, by Marj's rules, by the lack of space and oxygen. Most of all, by the lack of humanity. Being outside, in the fresh air, with no rules, was the perfect antidote. When I was too cold to take it any longer, I took my chances and walked back. It was just after 4am when I rang the doorbell and Marj thrust her angry head out of a top window.

"Don't think you can turn up here when the fancy takes you," she bawled. "It's not a bloody hotel! You can sleep in the porch."

"Please," I said wearily. "Please let me in. I'm frozen. I don't even have a coat."

But she snapped the window shut and that was that. I was just sinking to my knees, in the porch, when the door opened slightly.

"Quick," Kev whispered. "Get inside." We crept upstairs and, without thinking, I followed him into his room.

"Hope, you're icy cold," he said, taking my hands in his. "Come here, I'll warm you up."

We lay on his bed, on top of the covers, and cuddled. It was the start of an innocent romance; my first ever. Kev and I never slept together, we never went beyond a kiss and a cuddle. But he was kind and sweet and gentle. For his part, he loved the trouble I caused with Marj. He liked to see someone standing up to her. Our rows were entertaining for the other kids. I began running away more, on one occasion I even went back to the children's home and met Lara in the woods. It was harshly reminiscent of my meetings with Dougie, but I tried to push that from my mind. I always loved to see her, and it was the closest feeling I ever got to coming home.

"You need to look after yourself, Hope," she said. "One day, we'll get our own place, and we can do as we like."

"Yeah, and I won't be relying on a man next time around," I said. "I've learned my lesson."

Each time I ran away, it was Kev who waited loyally and snuck me back in, whilst the rest of the family slept. I loved and appreciated him more than he ever knew.

"You're one in a million, you know that?" I told him, sharing out the chocolates I'd nicked from the forbidden cupboard.

Cara and I were good pals too. She was worried about her unborn baby and frightened social services might take it away, after the birth.

"Girls in care never get to keep their babies, do they?" she said dolefully. "They never even give us a chance to prove ourselves. I want to be a mum. I want my baby."

An image of Tiffany, angry and sullen, invaded my thoughts. I wondered what had happened to her baby; it would have been born by now. A wave of debilitating guilt washed over me when I remembered how I had treated her. I'd had an affair with my friend's husband, my pregnant friend's husband. It was unforgiveable. I couldn't understand why I'd been so cold and cruel. I couldn't begin to tell Cara anything about Tiffany. She'd quite rightly be disgusted in me, just as I was disgusted in myself.

"I don't know, Cara," I said slowly. "I don't know anyone else from a children's home who's had a baby. I'm not sure if they'll let you keep it. But I hope they do."

Side by side in our twin beds in the darkness, we made lists of the baby names we liked. We totted up, mentally, how much it might cost to buy a cot, a pram, a highchair. She'd need baby clothes, nappies, formula milk, too.

"It's so expensive," Cara sighed. "It would really help if I had a bloke around. I can't do this on my own."

My thoughts turned to Dougie. Even though I never said his name out loud, he was a simmering and constant presence, an oily voice in my ear. Inexplicably, I missed him, or perhaps I missed the promises he had made. Certainly, I still grieved the life I'd thought I might have; the white wedding and the domestic bliss. And that sense of loss, the ache of an unfinished chapter in my life, only intensified as the months went on. In the lonely early hours, when I couldn't sleep, I hated myself for missing him. It was perhaps a version of Stockholm syndrome, where a hostage victim empathises with their captor. Dougie had physically never held me hostage or locked me away in a cell. Yet, emotionally I felt imprisoned, just as if I was chained to him. And though I hated this link, I craved it also.

Vulture-like, I picked over the bones of those nights at the derelict house. I loathed myself for not fighting back, for not at least speaking out, before we had sex. And that was how I saw it: we'd had sex. I believed I'd lost my virginity to Dougie, and I was embarrassed by it. It didn't once occur to me that it was a serious sexual assault on a child, it was rape, and it was against the law. No, if anyone was at fault, I felt sure it was me. For if I didn't want to have sex with him, why had I not run for my life, why hadn't I screamed at the top of my voice:

"No! no! no!"

I had said nothing. Not a word. My silence spoke volumes and it confirmed my complicity. I was to blame, just as much as Dougie, if not more. I had been so easily crushed and conquered. There had been no seduction, no bribery. Dougie had never once had to threaten me or use violence to make me do what he wanted. Neither had he ever bought me a present. He had never once taken me out for dinner. He'd never so much as got me a bag of chips. I didn't understand why that mattered so much to me. Yet it did. I was such pathetically easy prey. I was a little ladybug, quivering as I waited for a crow to swoop down and swallow me.

You are a little whore. You are a little slut. You are a little slag.

Absurdly, I was always afraid Dougie might track me down

and come after me. I worried he'd be angry. If it was my fault
– and I was sure it was – then he had every right to be furious.
Maybe he would find me and make me have sex with him again.
I shivered in bed and pulled the duvet tighter around me. When
I finally dozed off to sleep, I saw Dougie's four faces, just like
the Waterloo clock, each one sneering, treacherous, self-serving
and twisted. Suddenly, brutally, I was awake, drenched in cold
sweat, with my teeth chattering. What if he came for me? What
if he found me? What if I had to do it again? Yet there was
no suggestion he knew where I was, or that he even wanted to
know. I'd had no contact from him or Tiffany. My fears were as
irrational as they were crippling. Yet they felt so real.

"Hope, what's up?" said Cara, through the darkness. "I can
hear you shivering. Have you had a nightmare?"

"I'm alright," I mumbled. "You go back to sleep."

Despite my friendships with Kev and Cara, I was deeply
unhappy at the foster home. With the autumn nights of 1990
drawing in, I spent much of my day walking to and from the train
station in the dark, stumbling through fields and down roads
in the cold and rain. On occasions, Marj even drove past me,
with her own children sitting cosily in the back seat. She didn't
acknowledge me at all, despite me waving madly and running to
catch her car. She just acted as though I was a complete stranger.
Which of course, to her, I was. After her car had disappeared
from sight, I sank back against the hedge to catch my breath.

"Your make-up is disgusting!" I yelled, into the silence. "And
you're married to Worzel Gummidge!"

It didn't make Marj turn around and collect me. But it did
make me feel better. It made me smile, and smiling can never
be overrated.

27

ONE MORNING, at college, I began to feel unwell with a tell-tale pain in my throat and glands. Since I was small, I'd been plagued with bouts of tonsilitis which often left me too ill to get out of bed, and I recognised the symptoms only too well. By lunchtime, I was burning up with a fever and my neck was swelling. The college nurse looked at me in concern.

"Can we call your parents to collect you?" she asked. "I don't like the idea of you going home on public transport."

I shook my head wearily.

"No point," I said. "They won't come. They're foster carers."

The feeling of being completely alone in the world, of having nobody at all to care for me, was worse, far worse, than the tonsilitis itself. I didn't even have money to buy painkillers. The nurse did her best, but eventually, after she had failed to persuade Marj and Worzel that I was worthy of compassion, she paid for a taxi to get me as far as the train station. It was a small kindness, but it was one I would never forget.

"I have better things to do than come and collect you every time you flutter your eyelashes," Marj told me when I finally staggered in through the front door. "You need to learn that, young lady."

I gritted my teeth and said nothing. I felt too unwell to argue back. My postponed revenge came in short, sporadic bursts, when I helped myself to a little bit of her make-up, or I forced open the out-of-bounds cupboard to pinch all the Gold bars. It wasn't so much about the chocolate or her sacred Avon mousse foundation. I just wanted to get one up on her. It kept me going, it lit the spark inside me, knowing I had scored a small victory. But this was itself, in essence, a problem. Each victory was very small and very temporary. And after each minor lift, I was flooded with despair. I continued running away, sometimes overnight. I visited Marie, occasionally. I went back to see Lara. I even returned to the first children's home, in London. I went from one address to another, looking for my three brothers, or for old friends from the various institutions I'd lived in throughout my childhood. I was always trying to catch hold of something, always searching, but I didn't know what for. Never once though, did I look for my parents. One morning, dejected and downcast after a night in the cold, I called my social worker from the fostering agency, on the verge of tears.

"I hate it there and they hate me," I told him. "It's not home to me. It never will be."

He came to pick me up and when we arrived back at the foster home, Worzel had evidently had advance notice that the social worker was coming, because he had cooked me a full English breakfast.

"This is all for you," he smiled.

"You mean, this is all for show," I retorted, with something of my inner fire rising to the surface. "There's no way you'd cook me this if my social worker wasn't here. You don't even feed me."

Wurzel glared at me.

"Look around this kitchen," I said to my social worker, my indignation rising in my chest. "Two fridges, two sets of cupboards. All the decent food is locked away. I'm treated like an animal here."

I left them both standing there, mouths hanging open, and stomped off to my bedroom. I left the cooked breakfast untouched. Even though I was starving, it was more important for me to keep my dignity than it was for me to eat.

28

I HAD been at the foster home for three months when my social worker called to say the agency was taking my complaints seriously, and as a result I was being moved to another place.

"We've got a new home ready for you," he said. "It's part of the same scheme, for challenging children."

I felt that familiar buzz of excitement, followed by plunging doubt. I was thrilled to be getting away from Marj and Worzel. But there was no guarantee the new place would be any better at all.

"What's up?" my social worker asked. "It's a new start. It's what you wanted."

"Well, I've had plenty of those," I replied. "Each one delivers a bit less than the one before."

"This might well be your last chance," he warned. "You're 16 now, so if this doesn't go well, you'll have to go to a hostel."

His words struck terror into me. I knew all about hostels. The accepted trajectory, for girls like me, leaving care, was crappy hostel, crappy flat, crappy boyfriend. The hostels I'd heard of were riddled with drugs and trouble. That life was not for me. I didn't want any of those things. I did not want, above all, to turn into my mother. I made a conscious promise to myself, to stay out of hostels, and to survive. I had to make the foster placement work for me because a hostel was a risk I could not take. I was sad to say goodbye to Cara and Kev, and the two little girls. But I wouldn't miss Marj and Worzel. Not one bit. Before I left, I nipped into Marj's bedroom and slipped a half tube of her blasted Avon mousse foundation into my pocket.

"Just a little souvenir," I told myself.

It made me smile to think of Marj scouring her dressing table, emptying out her make-up bag, and screeching with rage when she realised it had been stolen. I knew too, that I'd never use it. It was all about me having the last laugh. Cara and I were both quiet as I carried my black bin bags downstairs.

"I hope you find a girl who deserves you," I said softly to Kev. "She's very lucky, you tell her that from me."

I kissed Cara's bump and told her: "Hold on to your baby, don't let them take her away. Promise me that."

My new foster home wasn't quite ready for me, and for a week or so I was shipped from one house to the next, spending a night here, a night there. I was so disorganised. Still, I reassured myself, if the new foster home wasn't ready, perhaps they were painting my bedroom or ordering me a new carpet. Despite myself, I began looking ahead, excited to meet my new parents. I was sucked into the trap of believing that maybe, just maybe, this one might work out. When the day finally came around, I was brimming with foolish optimism. It lasted just until the front door of my new home opened, and then the smell and the noise smacked me right in the face. It was like a double assault, and I took a step backwards.

"I think they have dogs," my social worker said, a little awkwardly.

"No kidding," I replied.

It turned out there were four dogs, a bulldog, a Boxer, and two crossbreeds. My new foster parents, Dot and Jeff, were an odd couple. Dot was tall and curvaceous with long, shiny blonde hair, and a laugh like a machine gun. She was wearing a tight leather dress, which to me, seemed the very height of glamour. Jeff was an ordinary looking bloke, memorable for two main reasons: his foul breath and his terrible haircut. I would later learn Dot insisted on cutting everyone's hair, and so the whole household was afflicted with awful hairstyles. She, naturally, went to a salon to have her own hair trimmed.

"Come on in," Dot smiled graciously, and again I was struck by how sophisticated she seemed. She wore beautiful make-up and lots of jewellery.

In contrast, the house itself was a disaster zone. It had gone beyond the point of needing a good clean and there were dust balls poking out from under furniture and nestling in corners. On one wall in the living room there was a row of paintings, depicting various breeds of dog, and they were encrusted with a thick layer of grime. But the sofa was soft and comfortable, there were lots of cushions, and a huge television. As Dot chatted with my social worker, I tried to remind myself to stay upbeat and buoyant. I knew I couldn't keep moving from one home to another, like a little cuckoo, always out of place, always unwanted. One too many in the nest. I had to make this work. Besides, I'd been warned. If this placement didn't work out, I was likely to be moved to a hostel.

"As you know, we never turn a child away," Dot was saying. "No kid is too bad for us."

I wasn't sure whether that was a good thing or not, particularly not the way Dot said it. I presumed social services excused the state of her home on the basis that she was too busy with the nobler task of rescuing the waifs and strays who nobody else wanted.

"Let me show you around," she suggested, standing up and smoothing the creases out of her dress.

My social worker said goodbye and I followed Dot on a bewildering tour of her home. Jeff, it turned out, was a DIY bodger who seemed to lose interest part way through every project. There were doorframes missing downstairs and a big hole in the wall. Upstairs, it looked as though he had tried knocking a bedroom through onto the landing and had given up, leaving a build-up of plaster dust and debris behind him. I'd never seen anything quite like it.

"Here's your room," Dot said, pushing open a door which was shorter than a standard door, and partially hanging off its hinges.

The room was tiny; there was just enough room for a single bed with a small table squeezed in at the end. There was no window, which was perplexing. I worked out Jeff had divided one large bedroom into three, slotting in dividing screens of plasterboard, and cutting out three separate doorways.

He had laid carpet tiles which did not fully cover the floor and they curled up at the edges, reminding me of the slices of stale bread I'd find in our kitchen cupboard, when I was small. The room was makeshift and had the feeling of a Portakabin more than a bedroom. I would later learn the requirement for children in foster care was a bedroom with a bed, wardrobe and desk. My new room did not even meet basic standards, and it was not a good start to my second spell in foster care.

Still, I balanced my portable TV from Issy on my table and unpacked my books. There was nowhere to store my clean clothes, so they stayed in the bin bag. I also had two big bags filled with dirty clothes. Because I'd been moved from one place to another, I hadn't been able to wash any clothes for over a week. Back downstairs, Dot ripped open the first bag and tipped my washing all over the kitchen floor.

"You dirty cow," she sneered. "Look at all this. Just as well for you that we take any kid here. Nobody else would have you, you know that."

A flush of shame crept across my face. My dirty clothes, even my underwear, were strewn across the middle of the filthy floor tiles, for everyone to see. Dot was right, I told myself. I was dirty. The evidence was right here.

"Sorry," I mumbled, scooping my clothes up in my arms. "I'll get it all washed."

Dinner was a plate of beige food, not dissimilar to the junk Marj had served up, but by now, I knew better than to complain. I was determined to keep my mouth shut. Afterwards, cheered by the thought of the comfy sofa, I went into the living room to watch TV. But a sharp voice pulled me back.

"Oh, where do you think you're going?" Dot asked. "Your living room is on the other side of the kitchen. You're not allowed in this one."

My good mood curdled. The foster children's living room was a hovel. It was freezing and the radiator was hanging off the wall. There was a plastic two-seater sofa, which was as hard as a brick, and a small portable TV. It could not have been more uncomfortable or unwelcoming.

"Think I'll have an early night," I sighed wearily.

Dot beamed at me, and it was more unsettling even than Marj's yelling. I couldn't for the life of me work out what there was to be so happy about.

As well as me, there were two teenage girls, Samira and Sharon, and a little boy, Harry, all in foster care. Dot and Jeff had two kids of their own too. Samira seemed quiet and troubled. She was in the room next to me, and I could hear her crying, long after the lights went out. The dogs slept in a makeshift shed which had been tacked onto the side of the house, but they barked and scrapped all night and kept me awake too. The next morning, there was no breakfast and nothing in the cupboards.

"Don't start," Dot said, before I had even said a word. "You want breakfast, you go out and buy some. And don't ask me for a door key either, I know your type. I'm not having you rummage through our stuff whilst we're out. You'd rob me as soon as look at me. If I'm not here, you're not here. Understood?"

I could have cried, not so much at Dot, but more at myself. I was so frustrated, so angry at myself for believing that perhaps this foster home might be different. I had built myself up for the sole purpose of Dot smashing me down again.

"Understood," I said flatly, reminding myself how horrible hostels were.

College was a bus ride away from my new home, and when I arrived, my psychology tutor pulled me aside.

"I'm really disappointed in you, Hope," he began, in a harsh voice. "You haven't been in for over a week, there's been no communication from you. No work submitted. It's just not good enough."

His words felt like the final straw. Everywhere I went, people seemed hell-bent on making my life unbearable. What was it about me? Why was I so easy to hate?

"I stayed in about six different foster homes last week," I replied quietly. "I didn't even know where I was going to end up or if I'd be coming back to college. I've just moved into a new foster home where I'm not allowed to sit in the living room, and I have to buy my own food. Finishing an assignment was the last thing on my mind. Sorry."

My tutor hung his head.

"I am so sorry," he said, falling over his words in embarrassment. "So sorry. I had no idea. Is there anything I can do? I really am sorry."

I shook my head and turned away. His kindness and empathy got to me far more than his outburst. I could cope with shouting and yelling. I was accustomed to nastiness and cruelty. But I was not used to goodwill at all, especially not from men, and it floored me completely. From then on, my psychology tutor was patient and thoughtful and offered me help whenever he could. But I couldn't ever look him in the eye because I knew his pity, reflecting back at me the hopelessness of my situation, would bring me to tears.

29

DOT, I soon learned, was Queen of cruelty. If Worzel, in the last place, had been Roald Dahl's Mr Twit, she was certainly one of Dahl's witches. Or maybe, I thought, The Wicked Witch Of The West from *The Wizard of Oz*. I had loved the film when I was little but had grown to hate it during my teenage years. 'There's no place like home' seemed like a spiteful jibe aimed straight at me. Even in my first few days, Dot made it her business to remind me – and everyone else – that she was the only foster parent in the UK who never turned a kid away.

"No kid is too bad for us," she boasted.

She repeated it, like an advertising slogan, every chance she got. Not only did it make me, and the other kids, feel absolutely desolate, but she also made sure it worked strategically in her favour. If any of us ever dared complain, or make an allegation about her, she could simply say we were so damaged that our claims had no credibility at all.

Nobody else will take these children! What else do you expect from them?

That first weekend I was there, Dot announced she was cooking us up a Saturday night treat. I didn't get my hopes up, but I was curious all the same. I stood at the kitchen door and watched her defrost a batch of cheap burgers. Then she got out a bag of flour and even from the doorway, I could see it was crawling with little insects.

"It's full of bugs," I shouted. "Look!"

Dot shook her head.

"They're just crumbs," she said dismissively, spooning the flour into a mixing bowl. "Silly girl. You need your eyes testing, Hope."

Did I? Was I going mad? But as Dot waved an arm to shoo me out of her way, I leaned in and got a closer look at the little black bugs scurrying through the flour.

"There!" I yelled.

"Oh, you're mad," she replied. "Quite mad."

"One of us is," I muttered under my breath. From a distance, I watched, revolted, as she mixed flour and lard to make a pastry and then wrapped it around the burgers. This, quite incredibly, was supposed to be our treat. Cheap burgers wrapped in lumpy pastry infested with bugs. Dot and her family, on the other hand, had steak, cooked and served separately. As she passed out the burgers on plates, she said:

"Enjoy the steak, kids!"

I found it almost impossible not to argue back. We all knew it wasn't steak. I didn't understand what her game was at all.

"The flour had weevils in it," I whispered when Samira took a bite. "Don't eat it."

She shrugged.

"Dot always cooks out of date food," she whispered back. "Nothing we can do about it."

The threat of a hostel loomed large in my mind, and I knew Samira was right. There was nothing I could do. Yet it disturbed me that Dot went to the trouble of wrapping the burgers in pastry and passing them off as steak. There was no necessity to do so. She didn't need to disguise the burgers and nor did she need to hide the fact that she and her family were eating steak. We were powerless to object, no matter what she fed us.

The pastry burgers seemed less of a money-saving exercise and more of a statement of power and control. It gave Dot a little kick to know she was feeding us pure rubbish, and that no matter how she goaded or teased us, we could not fight back.

"The steak was lovely," I told her, having slipped the burger into the bin. "I really enjoyed it."

I gave her what I hoped was a big beaming smile, similar to the ones she gave me. She knew I was lying. I knew she knew it. But if she wanted to play games, then I was happy to oblige. I might lose a few rounds, but I was determined to be the winner overall.

The following day, Sunday afternoon, Dot announced she was going to cut our hair. I watched, in morbid fascination, as she hacked first at her own sons' hair, then Harry's, Sharon's and Samira's.

"Oh no," I said firmly, dodging her scissors when she came for me. "Don't want my hair cutting. Thanks all the same."

There was a moment's silence, as if she was weighing up her next move. I levelled my gaze at her. I reminded myself I had come across much worse than Dot. She needed to know that. And it seemed perhaps my telepathy had worked, because in the next moment, she yelled: "Jeff!" and he came scurrying in, like a well-trained lab rat, for his hair cut.

"Sit still," she told him crossly, digging the comb into his skull and flexing the blades of her scissors.

Apart from his bodged DIY, Jeff seemed largely ineffectual in the family unit. If he had wrought as much havoc in his relationships as he did in his house, perhaps Dot might not have been so nasty and oppressive. As it was, he seemed as scared of her as the rest of us were. My minor run-in with her over my hair seemed to persuade her to leave me alone, in terms of physical abuse. Verbally, she was vicious. But she was never violent towards me. The other kids were not so lucky.

On a daily basis, I saw her lunging at them and battering them for no reason at all. Sometimes, it seemed as though she was itching to download her anger, and I wondered if her sole reason for fostering was so that she could explode at will and without consequence, on whoever happened to be there at the time. One afternoon, I came home from college to find a chunk of Harry's white-blonde hair pinned to the fridge with a magnet.

"Dot picked him up by his hair and pulled a clump out," Samira whispered. "It was dreadful."

"No!" I gasped, clapping my hand to my mouth.

The hair was a warning, a badge of honour, a trophy. Every time I walked past the fridge, I felt sickened that I had not protected him or defended him. Sickened that Dot could dole out such twisted punishment to a child. Sickened, most of all, by my own cowardice.

Even though I hadn't been there, I hated myself for not stepping in and stopping the violence. I saw it as my job to look after the other kids, especially the younger ones. And yet I was torn, dangling between two camps, holding onto each by my fingernails. I wanted to look after Harry. But I knew I could not risk going into a hostel. This hell, however bad it was, was not as bad as the hell which awaited me elsewhere.

Soon after his hair had been pinned to the fridge, Harry vanished, and another, older boy named Ned took his place. Just like everyone else, little Harry was swept out of my life, like a leaf down a grid.

30

ONE NIGHT, hearing Samira sobbing in the early hours, I crept into her bedroom, next door to mine. It was just as small and cramped as mine, and we had to huddle on her bed together.

"What's up?" I asked her. "You seem so sad. I often hear you crying."

Through her tears, Samira confided she had been sexually abused at home, by a family member.

"That's how I ended up in care," she told me.

My heart went out to her. No wonder she was so upset all the time.

"You should try and sleep," I said to her.

Back in my own room, I couldn't sleep either. I flicked on my portable TV, with the sound on low, and memories of Issy drifted back to me. She'd bought me the TV as a gift. I reminisced over our shopping trips and the day out at the theme park, smiling sadly as I remembered scrawling my initials on her wall.

It was almost too painful to watch the TV, because of the associations with my old life. It was nearly morning by the time I finally dozed, and even then, I could still hear Samira crying.

Downstairs, at the breakfast table, she looked exhausted. She was even more withdrawn than usual.

"Hurry up," Dot said impatiently. "I want you out of my kitchen. All of you. Buy your breakfasts on your way to school or college. Go on!"

When Samira didn't stand up, with the rest of us, Dot yanked her, by her collar, out of her chair and towards the door. My blood boiled, and it took all my self-control not to steam in and attack Dot myself. Instead, taking deep breaths and reminding myself about the hostel, I said calmly:

"Samira didn't sleep well last night. She needs a bit of kindness, that's all. You know what she's been through."

Dot laughed mirthlessly.

"What she's been through?" she scoffed. "You mean all her lies about being sexually abused? That's not true. She's a little storyteller, ain't you, Samira?"

Samira said nothing and, as I led her away, my arm around her shoulder, a throbbing rage threatened to burst out of me and spill all over. How could she get away with it? Dot's voice echoed down the hallway as we put on our coats and shoes, ready to leave.

"You're a little liar, pants on fire, Samira!"

Her machine gun laughter followed us down the path. That evening, I came home from a long shift at work to find Dot had pinned an announcement entitled: 'Eviction Notice: Hope Daniels' to the door of the fridge. She had used the same magnet which had held little Harry's hair in place. The notice gave me 28 days to leave. Mentally, I felt myself curling, like a ladybug, into a ball. But I knew I could not afford to show any weakness on the outside. My reaction to this was pivotal, in terms of the way Dot would behave towards me. Laughing, I scrunched the notice into a ball and kicked it across the kitchen.

"There," I told Dot. "That's what I think of your eviction notice."

Deep down, I was terrified of being thrown out. Horrified by the prospect of life in a hostel. But something told me it was better to play Dot at her own game, to meet her head on, but without getting embroiled in a physical or verbal battle which would end with me carted away to the dreaded hostel. The next day, there was another eviction notice on the fridge. This time, I ripped it into tiny pieces and chucked it into the air, like confetti.

"It's snowing!" I announced.

It became a battle of wills between us. Each time Dot posted an eviction notice, I came up with increasingly elaborate methods of destroying it. I fed one to the dogs. I floated one out of the window, like a kite. I drew a love heart on another and popped it on Dot's bed.

Eventually, the 28 days expired, and my social worker arrived for a meeting, bringing with him his manager. Dot showed us all into the posh living room and I noticed, with some surprise, she had put a framed photo of me on the sideboard. It was the first time I'd ever seen it.

"This is very serious," my social worker told me. "If Dot throws you out, you'll end up in a hostel, and you won't like that."

I was tempted to tell him exactly what life was like at Dot's, her temper, her violence, her cruelty. But I bit back on the words. He was right. I wouldn't enjoy being in a hostel at all.

"Dot," said the manager, as we all sat down on the comfy sofa, ready for negotiations. "Is there anything at all we can do to make you change your mind? We'd be so grateful if you would give Hope another chance."

Dot sighed melodramatically and began an Oscar-winning performance.

"I've tried so hard with her," she said, her voice laden low with sorrow. "You know I'd never normally give up on a child. I'll accept anyone at all here. But Hope, I'm afraid, is just unsalvageable."

She dabbed a few imaginary tears away with a tissue. The manager tried again.

"Please," he said. "Hope will behave herself, won't you? You're sorry, aren't you? We'd be really indebted to you, Dot."

Her face contorted as she wrestled with her dilemma.

"I can't see Hope out on the street," she said eventually. "You know me. I'm too soft. I can't turn a kid away. Go on then. One more chance."

There were handshakes and sighs of relief all round.

"You're a star, Dot," said my social worker. "One in a million."

She beamed modestly and I snorted quietly to myself in disgust. The whole show was quite clearly orchestrated, from start to finish. Dot pushed the 28-day notice to the absolute limit, to create maximum panic and drama amongst social services. Then, when she backed down, at the very last minute, she was lauded as a star and a lifesaver and Foster Mum of the Year. She fed off the attention like a leech.

"I see you," I said to myself. "I see you for what you are, Dot."

It was possible the social workers saw her true self too, and they simply played along with her performance, to keep her happy. It was glaringly obvious how manipulative she was. Yet I was not sure how useful my insight was. I felt confused by Dot's behaviour. She gaslit me and hoodwinked me and the fact that I recognised it was not helpful in me trying to prevent that. On the surface, she was a devoted foster mother, taking in the most damaged children who nobody else wanted. Yet scrape away, under the pastry layer, and she was as rotten as the weevil-infested burgers she cooked for us. After the social workers went home, she flung my photo into a drawer, and the living room was out of bounds once again.

"You remember, you're on your last chance," she told me, with a smile playing around her lips.

Next it was Samira's turn to receive the eviction notice. Her crime, apparently, was that she moped about and cried too much. Dot went through the whole charade again, waiting until eviction day until she magnanimously backed down, with a virtuous sigh, saying:

"I just can't turn a child away. I don't have it in me."

After Samira, it was Sharon. And then, it was back round to me. We all hopped on and off Dot's psychopathic merry-go-round, and her cruel eviction notices became a brutal but standard part of our lives. Often, I thought of how much I had looked forward to having foster parents, and how I had longed for this life. I realised, bitterly, how wrong I had been.

31

IN THE summer before my 17th birthday, Dot announced she was taking us all to Austria on holiday.

"Two weeks," she said excitedly. "A summer holiday!"

For holidays, and all other extras, the fostering agency paid out expenses. I was roped in, as the only member of the household who could calculate the claims, to fill in the necessary forms. It was a sizeable sum, to take us all to Austria, and the fostering agency had agreed to fund the trip for the four foster kids, me included. There were also claims for spending money, holiday clothes, even an overnight stopover. It really added up.

When I'd checked and rechecked my maths, I handed the form back to Dot, and, as her eyes lit up, my spirits dropped. I saw this exactly for what it was. I didn't have the heart to share my fears with the other kids, and yet it didn't seem fair listening to them planning their holiday, knowing how much they were looking forward to it.

"We are going, aren't we?" I asked Dot.

"Course we are!" she replied airily.

The cheque arrived from the fostering agency and Dot banked it that same day. The younger kids finished school, the summer holidays officially began, but there was no mention at all of Austria.

"Dot, what dates are we going on holiday?" Sharon asked. "It's just my cousin invited – "

Dot gave her a thwack on the back of her head, and she never got to finish her sentence.

"Stop going about the bloody holiday, all of you!" she yelled. "Or you'll get the back of my hand."

The holiday in Austria never materialised, and when my social worker asked if I'd enjoyed it, I nodded mutely. Dot and Jeff had a static caravan, about a half-hour drive away, and instead she took us there for a day out, that August. When we arrived, she and Jeff went off to the beach, with their two kids, and left me and the other foster kids to our own devices, on the caravan site. She left the caravan locked and refused to give us a key. But I was used to being locked out of places by now.

"I've left you some sandwiches under the caravan," she told us. "If it rains, you'll have to go and stand in the toilet block."

It wasn't quite a fortnight in Austria, but it was the best we were going to get. Dot was so impressed by my form-filling skills that she enlisted me to make more and more claims from the foster agency. One weekend, Jeff was putting his bike on the roof of his car, and he dropped it and smashed his car window. We all saw it happen. A few days later, Dot slapped a blank claims form and a pen down in front of me.

"Since you're so clever, I want you to write me an account of how Ned smashed the car window in a temper. Put his fist right through it. Remember that, don't you?"

Inside me, a small angry fist was clenched tight. But I nodded and did as she said, embellishing the details to impress her. When I read it out, she nodded her approval.

"That's another cheque on the way," she said gleefully.

From then, she made me fabricate claims for trips we never took, clothes we never bought, accidents we never had. It was galling, watching her defraud the agency and pocket all that money. She was already paid a generous fostering allowance, none of which she passed onto us. But there was absolutely nothing I could do about it.

One word from me, and I'd be fast-tracked into a hostel. I had no choice but to stay quiet. The plus side of Dot drawing me into her web of deceit was that she now saw me as an invaluable member of her gang. Neither she nor Jeff were particularly good at maths or English, so in her eyes, I was a real asset. She was in no way reasonable, or even civil, towards me. But the eviction notices stopped – for me, at least.

* * * *

I had been at Dot and Jeff's for around a year when I came home one day to find the place in uproar. There was a police officer and two social workers in the good lounge, along with Samira and Dot. Jeff was loitering outside the door, as though he had no business being there.

"What's going on?" I asked Sharon.

"Samira says she's been raped," Sharon replied. "She's in a real state."

I sucked in my breath. An image of Dougie flared across my eyeline; him looming over me, me lying on the bare floorboards of the derelict house. It was so vivid; I could even feel the bumps from the floor tacks in my lower back. Why would I think of that now? I tried to thrust it away.

"That's not the worst of it," Sharon was saying, in a loud whisper. "It was Ned. She says Ned raped her."

The shock zipped through me like electric.

"Ned?" I gasped.

I was dumbfounded. He was the newest member of the household, a boy in his late teens. I hadn't really spoken to him at all. I tried to stay out of the house as much as possible and most days I was either at college, at work, or with my mates. I rarely came back before bedtime, and usually fell asleep, exhausted, in the bath. It was Samira who always woke me, tapping on the door, gently encouraging me to get into bed.

"I can't believe it," I said. "Poor Samira."

She had been through so much already, being sexually abused before coming into care. The whole house knew about it, because of the way Dot had ridiculed her over it. And Ned would know too. Had he chosen her because she was an easy target, a victim? The wider implications, too, of us living in a house with a suspected sex offender were frightening. Again, like a sharp jab between my ribs, I thought of Dougie.

"What's going to happen? Has he been arrested?" I asked.

Sharon shrugged.

"Doubt it," she said. "It's just one kid in care abusing another kid in care. It's hardly headline news."

Depressingly, I had to admit she was right. When the meeting was finished, we were all called into the posh living room. I flopped down hard onto the cushions, knowing it would irritate Dot, but also knowing she couldn't scream at me with witnesses present.

"There's been a serious allegation about one of the male members of the household," said a social worker. "We had planned to remove the accused to a different address, but Dot has really kindly stepped in to say she will ensure the safety of you all. So it's been decided, whilst the offence is investigated by the police, that all males in the house must sleep elsewhere."

"It's so lucky we have the caravan," Dot butted in. "As you all know, I can never turn a kid away. I want to look after you all. So, Jeff and all the boys will be sleeping at the caravan every night."

It was such a ridiculous plan; I half thought it might be a joke. Firstly, how on earth would it protect Samira, or the rest of us? They were working on the basis that sexual assaults only took place at night. What was to stop us being attacked during the day? Also, I knew full well there was no way they'd stick to the agreement. It would be up to Dot, and nobody else, where the boys slept.

"We'll be back next week to see how it's all working out," said the social worker, and he and his colleagues picked up their shoulder bags and off they went.

Slack-jawed, I watched them drive away. They were either terribly naïve, or terribly negligent. I hoped it was the former. But the outcome would be the same, regardless. That same night, we went to bed as usual, and Jeff and the boys drove to the caravan. The second night, the same thing happened. But the third night, it grew dark and late, and nobody made a move. I went down to the kitchen for a glass of water and glanced uneasily from Dot to Jeff. I didn't dare mention the caravan, but I had worked out what was coming next. Sure enough, I saw Ned sloping into his bedroom as I was walking back upstairs.

"Why aren't you at the caravan?" I asked him.

He shrugged.

"Dot says, we're not going. Don't know why."

And that was it. After a couple of nights sticking to the agreement, it was abandoned. By decree of Dot.

"I don't want to sleep in this house," Samira told me tearfully. "I don't feel safe."

"Look, you can top to toe with me, if you like," I suggested. "Nobody will come for you with me there. Promise you."

We tried that for a couple more nights, though neither of us got any sleep. Then Samira's social worker visited. After speaking with Samira, he called us all into the kitchen.

"Samira tells me the males of the family have been sleeping in the house, as usual," he said. "Is that true? Did they go to the caravan? Or not?"

There was an uneasy silence. I could almost sense Dot rearing up internally, ready to strike out like a hissing snake at anyone who betrayed her.

"Well?" said the social worker. "Sharon, what do you say?"

Sharon hung her head.

"They went to the caravan, I think," she mumbled.

"Hope?" he asked. "Did they go to the caravan?"

I shifted uneasily from one foot to another. I wish I could say I did the right thing. I want to be able to say I stood up, in the middle of the kitchen, and I told the truth. That I protected Samira, and I spoke out against Dot and her tyrannical cruelty.

But I did not. I could not.

I looked at Samira's tear-stained face, her hands ripping a tissue to shreds, and I longed to help her. But the menacing spectre of the hostel dominated my thoughts. I could not go into a hostel. I could not become my mother.

"Yeah, they've been going to the caravan every night," I said shortly.

I could not look at Samira as I left the kitchen. Even as a child myself, I was disgusted by my own weakness. I despised my self-interest. But I did what I had to do. I hated myself for it, but I didn't regret it.

That weekend, Dot called me downstairs.

"I need you to fill in the claims forms for the trips to the caravan," she said.

"What do you mean?" I asked.

"Social services pay us an allowance, for Jeff and the boys to sleep there. We can claim back the petrol expenses too. I want you to work out the mileage. Claim for every night."

Her machine-gun laugh fired down the length of the hallway. Not only was she forcing me to lie for her, but now I was embroiled in her fraud too. It was a final twist of the knife.

32

SOME MONTHS – and no doubt several fat expenses cheques – later, Ned and Dot had a furious row in the kitchen. It was late in the evening, and so we were all at home.

"I will not have you eating my food!" she yelled at him. "Stay out of my cupboards!"

"I was hungry!" Ned roared back at her.

Dot was in the kitchen, and Ned was standing by the doorway. As they were arguing, Dot's younger son came running into the kitchen, through Ned's legs. He slipped on the greasy floor and knocked his head on the side of the table. I saw it all, and it didn't look like a serious accident. But a few days later, Dot cornered me.

"Ned's social worker is coming today," she told me, her eyes glinting menacingly. "When he asks what happened in the kitchen, you must tell him Ned pushed my son and he fell."

Frustration bubbled in my chest. But I said nothing.

"You hear me?" Dot hissed, grabbing me by the shoulders.

I nodded. Again, I felt furious at myself for lying for her. But I couldn't see any other option. The threat of the hostel, the fear and foreboding it triggered, was enough to make me comply. After we had all been interviewed by Ned's social worker, he left with Ned, and his mandatory black bin bags under his arm. I found the whole episode perplexing. Dot had the perfect opportunity to get rid of Ned, after he was accused of rape. Instead, she had insisted on him staying, only for her then to artificially manufacture an assault, so he would have to be removed from the house anyway. It was further confirmation that with Dot, it was less about logic and reason, and more about control. She was a bully, and she did things her way. Or else.

I would come across Ned, 20 years later, when he was begging on a street in London. He was scruffy and dirty, and living rough. But I recognised him immediately.

"I didn't push her son," he told me. "I've always felt wronged about that."

"I know," I reassured him. "I'm just sorry I didn't stand up for you."

Oddly, Ned told me he'd been back to Dot's, in the intervening years, to see if she would take him in again. Despite the way she'd treated him, he was drawn back there. It wasn't so difficult for me to understand. When you are used to nothing but abuse, it becomes normal, and sometimes, you seek it out.

After Ned came a younger boy, mid-teens, named David. He felt the sharp end of Dot's temper within a few days of his arrival and one morning, she threw all of his belongings into a large pile of building sand in the front garden, left over from one of Jeff's DIY cock-ups. She wouldn't allow him to put the clothes through her washing machine in case it got clogged up with sand. The poor boy left a trail of grit behind him for weeks afterwards.

Late in 1991, a few months after turning 17, I went into hospital to have my tonsils out. I'd been plagued by throat infections ever since I was a little girl, and my GP had finally decided they should be removed once and for all. Though I was anxious about the surgery, my main worry, going into hospital, was my lack of visitors. I knew nobody would visit me. There was no point in me kidding myself.

"You all comfy now?" the nurse smiled, as she tucked me into bed.

I nodded and smiled.

"Yeah, thanks," I replied.

I had the op, later that day, and by evening, I was back on the ward, dozy and groggy, and in need of a friendly voice. Visiting time came, and the girl in the bed next to me had such a cluster around her bed that the nurses told them to take it in turns.

"Two per bed," they said.

"Two per bed!" I said to myself. "I should be so lucky."

I watched, enviously, as they handed her little gifts, magazines and sweets. The girl on the other side of me had had her tonsils removed too, and she was quietly eating ice cream, whilst her mum sat beside her bed. My skin prickled with jealousy. I would have loved some ice cream, to soothe my sore throat. More than that, I would have liked a visitor. Most of all, I would have loved a mum. I held onto a faint hope that my social worker might pop in. But he didn't. And there was no chance of Dot or Jeff, or anyone else, making the effort.

"No visitors, then?" asked the nurse, unnecessarily.

"No," I mumbled, and hid my face in my pillow. At no time did I feel my loneliness more acutely than when I was ill. I had nobody. And sometimes, despite my bravado, that hurt.

33

I WAS around 17 and a half when, along with my friends, I started hanging around a local car park in the evenings, drinking cheap wine. If I wasn't at work, I'd go after college and stay until late. Dot didn't like us being in the house and I didn't like being there. My sole aim was to get as drunk as possible, as quickly and cheaply as possible, to blot out my thoughts for a while. Drinking seemed to be a miracle cure. It was a sure-fire way of blanking out all my anxieties and worries and I looked forward to that vague, woolly, feeling where nothing really seemed to matter too much.

I never linked this with my parents' addictions. I was a teenager, after all. Getting drunk was just what we did. One night, as I shared a bottle of wine with a pal, I got talking to Sam, a boy my age, who was part of the group. We didn't have much in common; he came from a nice, normal background, he'd had a pleasant, uneventful life. But we got on well, and soon started dating. He was my first serious boyfriend and inevitably, as our relationship became official, he asked if I would sleep with him.

"Yeah," I agreed, really on the basis that I didn't think I had any right to do otherwise.

Sam sensed I had reservations, but he had no idea of the reasons behind them. He presumed it was my first time, and that my inhibitions were the same as any other girl my age. I could not have told him about Dougie, about the horror and pain of those nights in the derelict house. Even if I could have overcome the shame, I just didn't have the words. Sam's parents worked full-time and so it wasn't long before we had a chance, one afternoon, to sneak out of college and let ourselves into his house. The whole experience, for me, was embarrassing and awkward. I squeezed my eyes shut and hoped it would be over.

"Wasn't so bad, was it?" Sam asked. "It'll get better, the more we do it."

I smiled but I knew there was no chance of that. Having sex was a means to an end. I did what I had to do. I had such low expectations from any kind of intimacy that simply getting through it was a success. Maybe being in a relationship emphasised the loneliness of my life in the care system. For as the weeks went by, I began to think about having a baby. The idea swirled around, before settling like a feather on me.

Ever since I was a little girl, I'd been adamant I would never have children of my own. My long-term goals: never to be a sex worker, never to be like my mother, never to be evicted, all seemed hopelessly unachievable, if I became a parent myself. My own experience of family life had been hideous. And neither did I want to bring a child into a society which had so abjectly failed me. My dream was to go to university, to study law or social care, and ultimately to help families like my own. Yet like most of my dreams, my plan seemed increasingly out of reach and insubstantial.

And yet, now I was almost 18, I could see with frightening

clarity that life was about to change, whether I liked it or not. I could not live with Dot and Jeff forever and neither did I want to. But I did not want to end up in a hostel. The girls I knew in hostels had sunk into serious drug addiction, violent relationships, prostitution and crime. A baby, I realised, could be my way around all this. And so, getting pregnant was a considered and a reasoned decision. I didn't feel in any way maternal. But I did feel scared of going out into the world, out on my own.

"What do you think?" I asked Sam. "Should we have a baby?"

I'd expected Sam might talk me out of it, but instead, he seemed all for it.

"Yeah, we could start trying straightaway," he grinned. "We could look for a place together. We'll get married if you get pregnant. I'd like that."

For the next part of my plan, I needed to learn to drive. I had been saving as much as I could from my wages at the shop, towards driving lessons. I booked in with an instructor who lived a couple of streets away, and as well as teaching me to drive, he and his wife befriended me. Looking back, I think I probably got more lessons than I paid for, and I passed my test first time. It was another stage completed. Another tick on my chart. And then, my period was late.

"I might be pregnant," I told Sam.

The flicker of uncertainty in his eyes was reflected back in my own. The reality, certainly, was different than the idea. We made an appointment at the family planning clinic, where my pregnancy was confirmed. I felt a little wobbly, as the nurse announced our news, but I reminded myself this was exactly what I wanted.

"You'll need to book in with your GP," she told me. "Have

you thought about which hospital you'd like for antenatal care? Where do you live? We could look at your options."

My mouth suddenly dried up. A greasy fear coagulated on my tongue.

"Oh, I'm not from round here," I stuttered. "I'll book in with my own GP, thank you."

I left as quickly as I could, with Sam, bemused, following behind.

"What's the matter with you?" he asked. "Why did you lie to the nurse?"

"I was just a bit overwhelmed," I said, conscious I was now lying to him as well. "Listen, can we keep the pregnancy a secret, just us for now, until I get used to the idea?"

Truth was, there was no way I could tell a doctor, or a social worker, or a midwife, that I was having a baby.

Girls in care don't get to keep their babies, we all know that.

I thought back to poor Cara. I wondered what had happened to her baby. I wondered about Tiffany's baby too. In spite of myself, I hoped Dougie had stood by her, in the end. Back at Dot's, I began preparations for the fight of my life. I had survived an appalling childhood; I had pulled through those harrowing years in secure units and children's homes. But this was a fight on a different level completely.

Now, I was battling to keep my baby. All night, I lay awake, making plans, as though I was going into war. I was due to meet my social worker later that week, to discuss funding for my studies, after my A-levels.

"I need to tell you about Dot and Jeff," I said, as we took our seats in a local café. "I never dared speak out until now."

If he tried to move me to a hostel, I had decided I would

215

reveal my pregnancy and wrong-foot him. He couldn't put me in a hostel, not with a baby. Instead, he said:

"This is such an important time in your education, Hope. I agree you can't go back there. This is very worrying. Let me see what I can to find you another temporary foster placement, just until after your exams. After that, you'll need to go into a hostel, until you get a university place."

"OK," I nodded.

I wrapped both hands around my stomach, and I hugged my secret close, like a soft blanket.

* * * *

Days later, I found myself edging past a gaggle of irate geese, who were guarding the gate to my new foster home. This was one battle I hadn't reckoned with.

"Hey!" I yelled. "Can someone help me out here?"

A man who looked like he had dressed in the dark ambled up the path, smiling. After scurrying past the geese unscathed, I had to pick my way through hens, cats and dogs, all milling around outside.

"We have an animal rescue centre," the man explained. "I'm Chris, and my wife's Felicity."

As he showed me inside the farmhouse, a pot-bellied pig waddled into the kitchen.

"A pig!" I gasped. "There's a pig! Get it outside!"

"She's a pet, she only has one eye," Felicity laughed. "She's harmless."

It wasn't often I was lost for words but being at the farmhouse left me dumbstruck. There were animals everywhere. Cats strolled luxuriously along the worksurfaces, there were dogs curled up snoring on the sofa. I even spotted a budgie flying around the bathroom. Later, I watched Chris loading horse-shoes into the dishwasher, alongside pots and pans. I groaned silently to myself.

My hygiene rules, made inflexible by the hovels I'd lived in as a child, were being smashed to pieces, one by one. Every drawer and cupboard in the house overflowed with clothes, tools, and general junk. The front door was permanently open with a draught flowing through the rooms, and yet there was an unmistakeable warmth about the place too, because Chris and Felicity's kindness extended beyond their animals and I was welcomed as one of the family, right from the start.

"You make yourself at home," Felicity told me.

As the days passed, I grew to understand the farmhouse was not filthy in the same way as Dot and Jeff's, or my childhood homes. It was earthy, at one with nature and animals. The cats and dogs, even the pig, roamed around the whole house, including the bedrooms and bathrooms.

"Out! I screeched, every time I found a smelly intruder, lying on my duvet.

Yet I couldn't find it in me to complain. Chris and Felicity were easy-going and relaxed, and perhaps we'd have got on well, given the chance. It was just such a shame I knew I wouldn't be there long. A couple of weeks later, my social worker came to see me again.

"I've got good news," he announced. "We've secured the funding for you to go to law school. You just need to get the A-level results."

As he spoke, his voice seemed to become softer and quieter,

until he had almost faded out completely. It was like watching a ship sailing away, until it was a mere speck in the distance.

"Hope?" he prompted. "What do you think?"

"I can't go to university," I said slowly. "I'm having a baby. I'm getting married."

It was his turn to fall silent.

"I can't believe it," he said eventually. "You were absolutely set on getting a degree. What's happened?"

I smiled weakly.

"Life happened," I said. "Just like it always does."

Sam and I were married in November 1992, by which time I was around three months pregnant. It was a hastily arranged ceremony, at the local register office. His parents paid for a buffet in the local pub. My social worker offered to drive me to the ceremony. The fostering agency paid for a bouquet. Everyone was very kind. I didn't have a wedding dress, but Sam had a friend who had recently got married.

"You could borrow that?" he suggested.

The problem was, she was a dress size 26 and I was a size 14. When I tried the dress on, it fell around me, like the folds of a collapsing tent.

"I look ridiculous," I said flatly.

But I had no other options. With hundreds of safety pins, I did my best to make it fit. The dress seemed, all at once, to symbolise the absurdity and stupidity of our decision to get married. I was in love with the idea of marriage, but I did not actually want to get married. I was desperate for my own Prince Charming to gallop into my life on his white horse. Yet if I was brutally honest, I suspected it wasn't Sam. I was fond of him, but I was doubtful about spending the rest of my life with him, and I imagined he felt the same. Neither of us could look that far ahead.

The morning of our wedding dawned, and I felt numb and empty. Subconsciously, I was disassociating myself from getting married, just as I did from all other trauma in my life. Because, yes, this was another trauma for me. But I couldn't find it in me to pull out. I didn't want to let Sam down either, or the people who had worked hard to make our day special. And besides, and most importantly, I had the baby to think of. I had made my decision, and I had to honour it.

"You can do it," I told myself. "Chin up, Hope, you've always wanted to get married."

But it was hardly the Cinderella wedding of my fantasies. On the journey there, I could barely sit down, because so much of the enormous dress was bunched up underneath me. The ceremony seemed generic and unromantic. And at the party afterwards, I watched people I didn't even know scoffing sausage rolls and knocking back vodka, and a feeling of utter desolation swept over me.

'What have you done?' I asked myself in exasperation. 'You've made a mess of things again. It's all your fault.'

In the days after the wedding, my social worker called to say he had found a little flat, which would give us a good start during my pregnancy. I would receive help with the rent and bills too.

"We want to support you, Hope," he told me. "I'll give you the address if you've a pen and paper handy."

But what I heard was:

"We want to keep tracking you, Hope. We want to take your baby away."

I played along, scribbling down the address, and thanking

him for his help. But before the wedding, I had already signed for a flat in a different area, and I was working double shifts at the shop, to pay for the deposit. There was no way I was going to tell him that.

"I'll pop in and see you next week, when you're settled," my social worker said. "Let me know if you need anything."

Without telling a soul, Sam and I moved into the flat I'd found. He didn't seem to mind the secrecy and deception; he certainly would not have understood it. But for me, this was about survival. I was convinced social services would take my baby from me if I stayed on their radar. There had been nothing to suggest that at all. Indeed, as a young girl, I'd shown myself to be very maternal with my younger brothers. But I had seen what happened to babies born in the care system. Girls like me were the under-class. You can barely look after yourself, never mind a baby! We were not cut out to be mothers.

Sam and I settled in well to the new flat and those first few months as newly-weds were special for us both. I loved having my own home, though I could not get used to owning a set of door keys. Never, in my entire life, had I been entrusted with keys and now, aged 18, I still did not feel deserving of such responsibility. Mostly, I left the front door unlocked, or simply hoped Sam would be in, when I got back from work. On the occasions I was locked out, I hung around outside, sheltering at the bus stop or under a shop doorway, just as I had in foster care. It was a habit I detested, yet I could not break it.

The final part of my escape plan was by far the most harrowing. To protect my baby, and to evade social services, I knew I had to cut myself off from all the links to my past. I could not risk contacting Marie, or Callum and Issy, or even Lara and my friends from the children's home. Even Sam, though he knew I'd been in foster care when we met, had no idea of my earlier life. It wasn't that I didn't trust him, or the others. I was just trying to minimise the potential for mistakes and slip-ups. I didn't want to put anyone in a position where they had to tell lies for me either. I didn't think I was worth that depth of loyalty.

Step by step, as my pregnancy progressed, I retreated into my shell as though I was preparing for hibernation. I was like a little hedgehog or a dormouse. There were parallels too, with the way I still hoarded food. I could not quite break those childhood hang-ups and I shopped every day, sometimes twice a day. My fridge was filled with fresh, healthy food and the cupboards were full. I bought far too much and inevitably, when the use by date passed, much of it had to be thrown away. Yet that, in itself, was a satisfactory part of the process. I took great delight in binning all the old food to make space for the new arrivals. It was a form of purging, emptying the fridge, ready for new stock. After growing up with havoc and crisis, I enjoyed keeping order.

I made sure I always had family bars of chocolate and countless packets of biscuits stashed at the back of the cupboards. Some evenings, I could polish the lot off in one go. My bingeing was very ritualistic, I would lay out everything I planned to eat, ceremonially unwrapping each bar before devouring them one by one. I grew accustomed to making myself sick, to get rid of the bloated, sickly feeling. And again, afterwards, I felt cleansed by purging. It was another form of self-harm, though back then, I didn't see it like that. For me, having supplies in, at all times, was like a comfort blanket.

Having food stacked up in the flat, knowing nobody from my

past could reach me, was at once reassuring and depressing. I needed the promise of a new start and yet I missed all the old faces. Each time I wobbled, I reminded myself that I had to disappear and become a new person completely. I had to forge a new past, as well as a future, and I had a very firm idea of how I wanted the world to see me; a normal wife and mother.

I craved anonymity and uniformity, for with it came respectability. I planned to wash my car on Saturday mornings and do my ironing on Sunday afternoons. I wanted a window cleaner and a milkman. I was excited by the idea of direct debits and water bills and insurance policies. I had it all planned out; I'd have two children, a boy and a girl, a husband who worked hard all day, and a neat little house in suburbia, exuding warmth and happiness. I clung to my childhood fairytale, gauzy as a gossamer strand, fine as Rapunzel's hair, flimsy as the wisp of a cloud.

I was giving birth, not only to my new baby, but also to a new me.

When my pregnancy reached five months, my bump swelled, and I sensed the first fluttering of movement from my baby. I loved to feel her wriggle and stretch. Since that first appointment at the family planning clinic, I hadn't seen a doctor, or a midwife, or any medical professionals at all. I hadn't had a single blood test, check-up or antenatal scan. Luckily, I seemed to sail through the pregnancy without any issues, but there were certain occasions when I really missed having someone to confide in. When my ankles swelled, and my back ached, I was desperate to call Issy or Marie. I longed for the reassurance of a mother figure.

"Is this normal?" I wanted to ask when I was kept awake

with indigestion each night. "Did you have this when you were expecting?"

And each time I almost peed myself when the baby sat on my bladder, I relayed the event, mentally, to Lara, imagining how much she would laugh.

'I can't believe you're pregnant," she'd have said. "You of all people!"

I could hardly believe it myself. I wanted so much to share my news with the people I loved the most, and yet I knew I had to remain focused. There was no chance of anyone finding me unless I reached out to them. It was way before the age of the mobile phone, and I didn't even have a landline in my flat. The only way to contact me was by letter, yet nobody knew my address.

My plan was foolproof. I should have been proud of my thoroughness. Yet I felt so lonely and far away. I might as well have been on the moon. Ironically, I thought by hiding, I was keeping me and my baby safe. I did not see that by rejecting all medical help, and cutting myself off from all support, I was potentially putting us both at risk. I was so convinced I was doing the right thing. I had two unshakeable instincts; my baby was a little girl, and she was going to be just fine.

"Mummy's here," I whispered, as my stomach rippled with her movements.

I had worked out she was probably due around May 1993. As the date drew nearer, I began plucking up my courage to go to hospital. When the labour started, I planned to turn up at the maternity unit, claiming to be new to the area. I could only hope they would not link me, through my personal details, back to my life in the care system. I had a new surname through marriage and hoped that would be enough to divert attention away from my past. May came, bringing warmer days, and I was exhausted. I could barely walk; I was so heavy. And then one morning, as I lay in bed, I noticed my baby was very still.

"Wake up, sleepyhead," I whispered, flicking my stomach.

But there was nothing. Immediately, I began to worry. I tried getting up and moving around myself, to see if that might rouse her. I had a bath too. But still, she was very quiet. My concern quickly ramped up to a state of panic. Frantically, I threw some clothes into a bag and took a taxi to the maternity unit.

"I can't feel my baby moving," I said. "Can you check her, please?"

"Where are your notes?" asked the midwife, frowning into her computer screen. "I can't find you on our system."

"I've been away, living overseas," I said. "Can you just check her? I'm worried."

In that moment, I wasn't bothered about being found out. I just wanted my baby to be okay. The midwife hooked me up to a monitor and to my relief, found a strong, steady heartbeat.

"Everything's fine," she smiled. "Don't worry. Baby was probably just asleep. What's your due date?"

I cringed and fumbled a response.

"Well, it looks to me like this baby has a couple of weeks to go yet," she said, measuring my stomach. "We'll book you in for a scan."

With my heart pounding, I gave her my details. I did not dare give a false name, knowing I'd later have to formally register the baby. I gave my married name, hoping she would not make the connection. But each time she typed another piece of information into the hospital system, I held my breath. I imagined her leaping from her chair and shouting:

"Hope Daniels! You're the girl from the foster home! The girl from the children's home! We've all been looking for you! You can't keep that baby!"

But incredibly, she finished booking me in, and said nothing at all. I was safe for now, at least.

"We got away with it," I whispered, patting my bump. "Nobody suspects a thing."

Much later in life, I would learn I was wrong. At the start of my pregnancy, the family planning clinic had alerted social services, and also my GP, and they had all been trying to trace me. My medical notes were filled with details of their attempts to make contact. They had been to my old flat, even to my old place of work, to try to track me down. I was running away from the same people who wanted to help me. Problem was, I could not be sure what kind of help they had in mind.

34

THE SCAN showed I was carrying a little girl. I'd known it, right from the pregnancy test, but it was so exciting to have it confirmed, and to see her tiny little limbs on the screen. She gave a little hiccup, and my eyes misted over with love.

"Mummy's here," I murmured.

On June 18, my contractions began, and Sam and I went to the hospital. Twelve hours on, and with my labour progressing slowly, I was in agonising pain. I clung onto the gas and air as though my life depended upon it.

"We're going to examine you, check how far along you are," the midwife announced.

A male doctor walked into the delivery suite and rolled up his sleeves. Dizzy with pain and drugs, and with the sterile smell of the hospital a sharp reminder of the secure units, I became disorientated and confused. Through my haze, I saw Dougie's face, superimposed onto the doctor's body.

"Get away from me!" I yelled. "You're not taking my baby! Leave her alone!"

With a huge effort, I tried to pull myself back to the present. But I felt weighted down by the chains of my past. On June 19, my little girl, Lucy, came into the world, perfectly healthy and absolutely beautiful. I was overcome with a love I'd had no idea existed. As I held her in my arms, I felt a devotion so fierce, it blazed like a fire within me.

"Let me take the baby for a moment," said the midwife, scooping her out of my arms. "You have a tear; we need to get you stitched up."

The same male doctor walked back into the room, and again, it was a vivid and terrifying apparition of Dougie walking towards me; right down to the casual, sloping gait and the cock-sure smile. I had always known he would track me down. And here he was. In the cruellest twist of all, he was here to take revenge, not on me, but on my baby daughter.

"Get out!" I shrieked. "Get out! Don't come near her!"

Arms and legs flailing, I could hear piercing screams which I didn't even recognise as my own.

"If you don't settle down, we'll leave you unstitched," snapped the doctor. "Keep still."

My delusions swung violently from 1988 to 1993 and back again. I was nauseous with fear and confusion. My hair was plastered to my face with sweat, my whole body tensed and terrified. Sam was by my bedside, but he had no idea what was wrong with me. I could not confide in him about Dougie; not then, not ever. I thought he'd leave me if I told him the truth. Worse, I thought he would despise me.

"Calm down," said the midwife softly, taking my hand. "You're safe here, Hope. The doctor is trying to help you."

Somehow, the medical team managed to get my stitches done and Sam went home. Afterwards, I was left on my own with Lucy. Cradling her, smelling the newness of her scalp, marvelling at her tiny nose, I felt like the luckiest girl in the whole world.

Yet instantly, my joy was clouded by self-doubt. Did I deserve her? Could I really look after her? Perhaps social services would be right to take her away from me. I had, after all, evaded all antenatal care, right to the last minute. I had potentially put her at risk. My behaviour so far as a mother was naïve and erratic. My own parents had failed miserably at the job; what if it was genetic? What if I was the same? I stared at her sleeping face, and I felt so helpless, so inadequate.

It was probably no co-incidence, either, that the spectre of Dougie, the ghost of my past sins, had appeared during the birth. He was here to remind me that I was not fit to be a parent. I'd had an affair with a married man, the husband of my pregnant friend. I was the lowest of the low.

As the night wore on, my thoughts ran riot, knotting and tangling like balls of wool. I felt more and more convinced that I was just not worthy of being the mother of such a precious and perfect little individual. She was unsullied, unstained, pure as freshly falling snow. I was damaged, tainted and broken.

How could I ever have thought I could be mother to this little girl? She deserved so much better. All through the early hours, and into the next morning, I was plagued by graphic flashes; the half-eaten bird outside the derelict house, Dougie's yellowy fingertips as he shuffled the cards for strip poker, the old man with the pornographic film and the sticky sofa. I sat up and looked at my daughter, snuffling softly in her hospital cot, her cheeks impossibly smooth and soft.

"I'm sorry," I murmured, through my tears. "I'm so sorry. I thought I deserved some happiness. I thought I deserved you. But as usual, I was wrong."

Later in the day, a midwife drew the curtain around my bed and pulled a chair up to my bedside. Cuddly and pillowy, she reminded me of the cooks back at the children's home. She had black skin and brown eyes, filled with tenderness.

"How are you getting on? Feeding, sleeping? Any problems?"

I didn't reply.

"If I show you how to change baby's nappy and give her a wash, we could maybe think about you going home later."

I stared at her.

"With the baby?" I stuttered.

"Yes, with your baby," she beamed. "Of course."

As she fussed around me, looking for a new outfit and a nappy for Lucy, I felt fat tears rolling down my face and plopping onto my hands. I felt so melancholy, so sad and confused.

"What's the matter, darling?" asked the midwife. She put down the nappy and sat on the bed, next to me.

I shocked myself as the words fell, scalding, from my lips.

"I am infected," I sobbed. "I'm a little slag. I'm a slut. A whore I can't take this baby home."

The midwife put her arms around me, and I laid my head on her chest and wept.

"You are going to be a wonderful mummy," she told me. "Believe in yourself. You are going to take this little girl home and you are going to be fine."

She could never have known what impact a few moments of kindness would have. I stored her words in my soul, and I drew on them, at my lowest times.

****

Despite the compassion from the midwife, taking my baby girl home was daunting. I adored my daughter. I idolised her. But emotionally and practically, I felt woefully inadequate and lacking. I had no idea at all how to look after a newborn baby. I didn't know how often she should be fed, or how to get her wind up. I'd not a clue how long babies should sleep for.

"We're going to be okay, you and me," I told her, as I settled her in a cot at the side of my bed. But the words were more for my benefit, than hers.

I had no support around me, no advice from friends or relatives, no contact with anyone from my past. Instinctively, after giving birth, I wanted to share the news, I wanted the whole world to admire my beautiful daughter. I longed to announce her arrival, trumpet it from the rooftops, sing it from my windows. Yet though I was sorely tempted, I knew I could not take the risk. I didn't tell anyone, beyond Sam's immediate family, that I'd given birth. Instead of basking in the warm glow of motherhood, I hid myself away and tried to pretend I did not exist.

My main enemy, above friends and family, was the authorities. I had to keep social services away; they were a wolf at my door, fangs dripping, waiting to pounce. The hospital had arranged follow-up visits from the midwife and health visitor, but I had the bare minimum of contact. They seemed content just to weigh Lucy and check her over, and they never asked about my background. I didn't volunteer anything either.

Certainly, I never admitted to having been in care. It felt like the ultimate shame, like revealing I'd been in prison for murder. I carried the secret with me, and it ate away at me, burrowing deeper and gnawing at my insides, leaving me raw and exposed. Memories of Dougie bubbled and festered at the edge of my consciousness. It was an open wound, and every time it started to scab over, a fresh memory made it bleed again. I didn't understand why thoughts of him bothered me so much and why I was so hung up on those nights in the derelict house. I did not allow myself to examine the significance and instead, I focused on my darling little girl.

On a steep learning curve, we fell into something of a routine. I didn't dare ask anything of the community midwife, in case she suspected I couldn't cope, but I watched her closely; the assuredness with which she picked my baby up, the expert manner she dressed and undressed her, the confident way she cradled her in the crook of the arm. They were all little tips which I committed to memory. As the days passed, I settled more and more into the role of being a mother.

"I'm getting the hang of this," I told her with a smile, but deep down, again, I suspected I was trying to convince myself, more than her.

At around four weeks old, Lucy began crying a lot. She didn't seem to feed well, and she lost a little bit of weight. Much as I hated to draw attention to myself, I was worried, and I called my health visitor. When she arrived, she asked me to show her my feeding routine, and immediately, the milk from the bottle splashed all over Lucy's little face.

"This always happens," I complained.

"Let me see," said the health visitor.

She peered at Lucy's bottle and smiled.

"You have the wrong size teat," she explained. "This is the one for toddlers. That's why Lucy is losing weight and crying so much; she's not getting her milk."

I burst into tears.

"This is all my fault," I wept. "I didn't even know there was such a thing as different sizes of teat. She could have starved."

"I think it might be best to get you both checked over in hospital," the health visitor suggested. "Just to put your mind at rest."

"No," I protested, an upsurge of fear in my throat. "No, I can manage. We're okay, honestly."

But the health visitor was already dialling the hospital.

"I can drop you off there now," she smiled. "Just for checks."

But all I heard was: "I can drop you off there now and we're going to take your baby away."

Lucy and I were admitted to hospital, into a room of our own. I felt very much like a little goldfish, swimming round the same, restrictive bowl, with a big, judgemental nose pressed up against the glass and a pointy finger tapping on the rim.

Oh she can't put a nappy on straight, can she?

Why is she singing that same dismal lullaby?

That's the girl from the children's home, I'm sure of it. She should not be in charge of a child. No way.

I hardly slept at all. I was certain, at any moment, social workers would rush in to take my baby away. Just as I had been taken from my own mother. But three days on, a doctor came in and said:

"Well, your daughter is gaining weight now. You both seem much more settled. Would you like to go home today?"

I was so overcome with relief and happiness; I could have hugged him.

"Thank you," I said, dropping my head, heavy with stress, into my hands. "We would love to go home. You don't know what this means to us."

35

AS SOON as I arrived back at the flat, I called the landlord to give notice, and began looking for a new place. The medical staff had been professional, fair and kind, and yet the hospital visit had only made my paranoia worse. I just could not dispel my suspicions that next time, they would take my baby away.

"We're off to a new place," I told Lucy brightly, as I packed up her cot and her toys. "Won't that be fun?"

Within a month, we were living in a new place. I told nobody where we were. I knew, eventually, I'd have to register with a doctor, a dentist, a nursery. But I was hell-bent on putting it all off for as long as I could. It was like being on the run and it was exhausting. One day, out shopping with the pram, I thought I saw my health visitor, from behind. She had the same swinging ponytail and seemed to be wearing a similar coat. I ducked behind a shelf, my legs weak with fear. When I finally dared to peek out, the woman turned around, and it was a complete stranger. I was living like a fugitive, terrified of being tracked down. I needed help, I needed support, yet I was shutting out the very people who were offering it to me. I stuck firmly to my resolve to cut ties with everyone from my past. And in addition, I was wary of making new friends too. I worried about people prying into my background and asking questions about where I'd come from and who I was. I carried my secrets around like rocks in my pockets and they grew heavier and heavier as time went by. The shame dragged me down, spreading and ulcerating. It was so strong; I could almost smell it. I thought back to the stench of my childhood home, the urine, the sweat, the stale booze. I had internalised that smell, and I was carrying it with me, everywhere. Much as I tried to reinvent myself, the smell gave me away. I could not escape my past and I had been foolish even to attempt it.

You are a little slag. You are a little slut. You are a little whore.

On the outside, Lucy was thriving. She hit all her milestones, and she was a contented, cute little girl. I became more in tune with her needs and more experienced as a mother. Yet my own needs were beyond me. I still did not feel I deserved this beautiful baby. I could not believe she was mine. Sometimes, when she was sleeping, I'd peer over her cot and her perfectness took my breath away. I felt a bloom of love so powerful that it terrified me. And so instead of enjoying motherhood, I was frightened by it. I felt certain it would not last. Certain I would be outed as an imposter. There was a sense of togetherness, a sort of siege mentality, holed up in the flat, just me and my baby, like escaped prisoners. Yet I also felt sadly and tragically alone.

When Lucy was 12 weeks old, she had her second set of vaccinations, and the nurse at the clinic was especially chatty, asking if I had other children, and if my parents were a good support to me.

"Why?" I replied sharply. "Why do you ask about my parents?"

"No reason, love," she said, "It's just nice to have a granny and grandpa, that's all," and she moved onto the next patient.

But her questions had freaked me out. When I got home, I gave notice on the tenancy, and I began packing. We were no sooner settled in our new place when Sam's extended family began persuading us to get our daughter christened.

"It means a lot to my family," Sam said. "They're very religious."

Without thinking it through, I agreed. But then, to my horror, I was presented with a guest list, catering options, choices of readings and hymns.

"You need to make a list of your side of the family," Sam said. "Who would you like to invite?"

My mind swam with visions of Issy and Callum. I knew how proud they would be.

"Okay," I relented. "I'll invite two people. But that's all."

Issy was thrilled to hear from me when I called.

"What!" she squealed. "You've had a baby girl! Oh, Hope, why didn't you tell us? We've been so worried about you."

She wanted to come over, that very minute. And when she did visit, for the christening the following weekend, she brought clothes and little gifts for Lucy.

"She's beautiful, she's the double of you," Issy beamed, and I swelled with pride.

As they left, Callum said, "You must stay in touch now. Your social worker has been trying to contact you too. We've all been worried."

His words sent a chill through me, but I managed a sort of smile. The day after the christening, I began looking for a new flat. And that's how it was. Each time I got spooked, each time

I saw a health professional, or I met someone from my past, I moved house. I packed stuff for Lucy and for Sam, but mostly I didn't bother too much about belongings for myself. For me, moving house was just part of a natural process. It was like shedding a skin or coming out of a chrysalis. Over a period of three years, I moved seven times. We didn't put down roots, we didn't make friends, we didn't register our presence with anyone. Looking back, I wonder whether it was about more than simply moving to evade detection. Perhaps I had to keep moving because I was running away from myself.

36

BEFORE LUCY'S second birthday, I fell pregnant again. Our baby was planned, and I was keen to have a sibling for my little girl. On the outside, I was hell-bent on creating a façade of married respectability, a sort of maternal utopia. I hankered after my vision of two children, one boy, one girl, a happy home, a happy marriage. I refused to admit, even to myself, that it was all a sham.

I had let the authorities into my life a little. But as soon as I found I was pregnant, I closed up again, like petals on a cold night. Again, I became obsessed with the idea that they would take my baby away. I went through almost the entire pregnancy without so much as a scan, or a blood test. I did not even register with a GP, never mind a maternity hospital.

My second pregnancy went well, but it was harder, because I was running around after a toddler too. I would have appreciated advice from other mums, even if we were only moaning about sleep deprivation or morning sickness. But I knew I could not risk attending the local toddler groups or joining the mum and baby sessions. I was sure to be found out if I started mixing in those circles. Yet worse than the lack of sleep, the pregnancy symptoms, the toddler tantrums, was the loneliness. Sometimes, with Sam at work, I felt the cold fingers of isolation curling around my neck, and they scared me.

Without my brain really giving permission, I found myself in the phone box at the end of the street, dialling Issy's number. As it rang out, I leaned back against the door, and I had a sudden, savage flashback. Once again, I was standing in the phone box, outside Dougie's flat, reversing the charges back to the children's home.

I'll say this for you girl, you give good head.

The desire to stand under a hot shower, to scrub myself clean, was overwhelming. I didn't want these reminders, not now, not ever, but especially not when my daughter was holding tightly onto my free hand and my unborn child was kicking in my stomach. I could not have my old life leaking into the new, infecting my role as a mother. It would be like pouring acid into custard. I wanted Dougie as far away from my new family as possible, but no matter how fast and how far I ran, he always seemed to catch me up.

"Hello, anyone there?" Issy was saying.

Her voice punctured my thoughts and I heaved myself back to the present.

"Sorry," I stuttered. "It's me, Hope. I wondered if I could come and see you. It's been so long, and I just need to see a friendly face."

"Course you can," Issy replied. "Come right now. I can't wait."

Before I hung up, I made her promise not to ask me any questions about where I lived and not to push me into contacting social services. I knew I was putting her in a difficult position, but I also knew she wouldn't let me down. We spent a wonderful afternoon with Issy and Callum, still living in the same house as all those years earlier. They were thrilled to see how Lucy had grown, and excited I was expecting another baby.

"Please, stay in touch," Issy pleaded, as we said our goodbyes. "I won't tell a soul I've seen you. I promise you that. I just need to know you're alright, Hope."

On the bus journey home, I felt stronger, brighter. Seeing Issy was a pick-me-up, an infusion of happiness. I would keep this in reserve and rely on it, the next time I was feeling low.

Towards the end of my pregnancy, I noticed the baby had stopped moving so much. It was just like the first time, but that gave me no reassurance. I needed to know my baby was alright. I packed a hospital bag, and Sam took Lucy to his parents' house before joining me at the maternity unit. The idea of Lucy being looked after by someone else, even by in-laws, was almost more frightening than the prospect of giving birth. The midwife booked me in, and I faced the usual inquisition.

"You should have been in to see us before now," she frowned, flicking through her computer. "I can't find anything on your records since your first child. Where did you have your antenatal scans?"

I shrugged apologetically and made a mental note to move house again as soon as the baby was born.

"Sorry, I've been living abroad for a while," I said. "I did mean to register with you by now, I'm sorry, I really am."

Outwardly, I was so polite and compliant. Inwardly, I was suspicious of everything. I was sent for a scan and for a moment, all my worries were swept aside by that magical moment of seeing my baby for the first time.

"The baby looks fine, good strong heartbeat," said the sonographer, as she pointed to the screen. "I think he's just lazy!"

I beamed.

"So I'm having a boy?" I asked. "That's wonderful. Thank you."

My son Jake was born in May 1996, and he was beautiful. A sense of fun and mischief shone out of him, even as a tiny baby. He was so alert, his eyes scanning the room, his arms up and down in the hospital cot, like sails on a miniature windmill.

"I can see you're going to keep me busy," I smiled. "Welcome to the world."

The birth itself, and also taking Jake home, was far less traumatic this time. But when he was just a few weeks old, Sam and I separated. Our relationship had been rocky for some time and we both felt it was for the best. In truth I had married him more for *what* he was, than *who* he was. We were young, immature, neither of us ready to commit to a lifetime together. We parted as friends.

Yet on my own, with two little ones, I floundered. I was in the grip of what I would later learn was severe postnatal depression. Everything felt like such a task, as though I was wading through cold, thick treacle in my slippers. It was a huge effort just to get myself out of bed each morning. I was only 22 years old, yet I felt like an old lady, with my batteries almost used up.

And still, I was convinced that my babies would be taken away from me, that social services would knock on my door and demand I hand over the most precious things – the only precious things – in my life. I knew I could not live with myself if I lost them. I kept on moving, every few months, but I knew also that our nomadic lifestyle could not last. Lucy was due to start at nursery, she needed a settled home, a solid base, and friends of her own. These thoughts petrified me.

And if not the social workers, then I was certain some other bogeyman would come to snatch my children. I did not deserve my babies, I was not worthy of being a mother, and I feared, eventually, I would be found out. A cot death perhaps. A road accident. Maybe I'd lose them to meningitis, sepsis, or childhood cancer. What if they were snatched by a paedophile? Or a murderer? Or Dougie? The fears whirled inside my head like a blizzard. Within the confines of my mind, I catastrophised constantly. I could not push the pram down the street without visualising a car mounting the pavement and wiping us out. I could not open the window an inch on a sunny day without imagining Lucy plunging to her death on the street outside. My imagination ran riot with accidents, illnesses and crimes. The wait, and the weight, of the expectation, was exhausting. Just being myself, coping with these thoughts, was as much as I could manage. Yet of course, I had to show, outwardly, that I was capable. I had to be compliant and co-operative. Because one chink in my self-control, one small sign that I was cracking, and I knew social services would pounce, like a cat on a poor mouse. And I would never see my children again.

As I child, I had always vowed to be open, brave and honest; I was determined to be nothing like my mother. Yet I was losing every argument I had ever made against her. Murky secrets swirled around me, just as they had around her. I was chipping away at the person I wanted to become, even before she had taken shape. And perhaps, if I did not have the courage to own my past, then I did not deserve a future. It was my fault that I was in this predicament. Again, my thoughts circled back to myself. Again, I was to blame.

* * * *

When I could postpone it no longer, I finally signed Lucy up to start at nursery. The thought of her being away from me, for so long, was intolerable. Instead, I volunteered to help out at nursery myself. That way, I could keep a close eye on her all day. I was allowed to take Jake along with me too.

"We'd like you to pitch in generally, putting on coats and shoes at playtime, encouraging the children at tidy up time. That sort of thing," the teacher smiled.

"Perfect," I replied.

On the surface, I looked like a normal mother, eager to give something back to the community. And on one level, that was true. But the fear that followed me around betrayed my darker motive. Even whilst I was playing in the sand or skipping with the other children, my eyes were always firmly fixed on my daughter. I panicked every time I lost sight of her. Mini disaster films played over and over in my mind; I imagined a social worker bursting into the classroom and taking her away.

I worried about paedophiles snatching her from the play-ground. What if there was an earthquake and the ground swallowed her whole? I slowly realised that being with my children every moment of the day was making my paranoia worse, not better. It was not good for me and, certainly, it was not good for them. Motherhood was about learning when to hold on. But also when to let go.

In the emotional shelter of our own home, I worked hard at

being the best mum I could. Yet each milestone, each occasion, was tinged by sadness. Being a parent myself brought into sharp focus the failings from my own childhood, and I suffered graphic, technicolour flashes from my past.

When I read Lucy a story, I remembered my own fascination with fairytales and happy endings, and I was enveloped by feelings of deep sorrow. Tucking her under her princess duvet at night, I remembered my own filthy bed, still wet from the night before, positioned so I could see Mum's punters at full throttle. In the mornings, as I made Lucy's breakfast, I saw my four-year-old self, opening bare cupboards, peering into an empty fridge, and realising I would have to go hungry. I was tormented, haunted by my own childhood ghost.

Overwhelmed with pity and sadness for the lost little girl I had been, I was also consumed with layer upon layer of anger and resentment towards my parents. Now that I understood what it was to be a mother, now that I had embraced the responsibility and the immense privilege, I was livid at the magnitude of their failure. The only way I could block out my fury was to drink. As a teenager, I had loved the cotton-wool numbness which alcohol brought with it, and I yearned for my head to be empty again.

When the children were in bed, and only when I was sure they were asleep, I'd open a bottle of wine. One guilty bottle a night soon became two, and then three. I hit the Bacardi too. The addiction crept up on me, like a sneak thief, in just the same way I had skulked around the market stalls, when I was out stealing. Yet to my dismay, this time around, the alcohol seemed to have the reverse effect. Getting drunk only triggered my trauma and every night I was chased down and persecuted by visions from my past.

I'm becoming an alcoholic.

I'm turning into my mother.

I am a little slag, I am a little slut, I am a little whore.

I was terrified of being found out; paralysed with fear that my children would be removed. Social services would have every right to take them away, I reminded myself. Yet irrationally, that admission made me angry. How dare they tell me what was best for my children? My children. It was a vicious circle, and the more anxious I became, the more I drank. I was on a hamster wheel, pedalling furiously and I knew my energy could not last.

37

WHEN JAKE was around six months old, I was assigned a new health visitor. She called round, unannounced one afternoon, just as I was preparing food for the children. To the outside world, it was a typical domesticated scene. Yet the kitchen bin was rattling with empty wine bottles, and my head was rattling with unease.

"Is everything okay?" she asked kindly, as she took a seat in the living room. "It's just we haven't seen you at the clinic for a while."

I said nothing. I could not trust myself to speak.

"I love your flowers on the windowsill," she commented. "Each time I drive past, I notice you have fresh flowers at the window, and it makes me smile. I always think this must be a nice place to live."

The compliment was so unexpected, and, in my view, so undeserved, that I burst into tears. The words which followed rushed from my mouth and burst, like a bubble, in the air around me.

"I'm not coping well at all," I confessed. "I don't feel like I'm a good mum. I drink too much. I have so much baggage. I was in care myself when I was little. I'm convinced you're going to take my kids off me. There, I've said it now."

Each word was like gun shot, piercing me deeply. Part of me expected her to call for reinforcements and to remove the children, there and then. Instead, in bizarre understatement, she just smiled.

"I think you probably need a bit of support, that's all," she said. "There are no concerns at all about your capability as a mother. Please don't worry about that."

The relief was like the biggest wave, washing right over me and my children, and leaving us standing, with our heads held high. For the first time, that afternoon, I really engaged with the people who had been trying to help me for so long. The health visitor, whose name was Amy, gave me a book called 'Toddler Taming'. She also left me with a new fireguard and some tips on getting Jake to sleep through the night.

"You're coping with a lot," she said, as she stood up to leave. "You should be patting yourself on the back, Hope, not beating yourself up."

Amy arranged also for a Homestart volunteer to come round once a week. She in turn offered help with practical tasks but what I really valued was the emotional and psycho-logical support. I loved just sitting and chatting with another mother, listening to her advice and her experiences. The depression was still there, lurking, and I continued to drink in the evenings. But it was manageable, I told myself. It was all under control.

The months passed, Lucy started school, and again, I was reluctant to pass her into the care of the teachers. I volunteered to help out in class, but I was only required one day a week. I signed up for all her school trips too. But none of this felt like it was enough. Each morning, I lingered in the playground, delaying my final goodbye. Eventually, her teacher called me into school.

"I'm sorry, we can't have you waiting in the playground each morning," she said. "The children need to settle. You will have to drop your daughter off at the gate instead."

I stared at her incredulously.

"Are you saying I'm actually not allowed in the playground?" I asked.

"I am," she said. "It's for the best. Please don't take it personally, we have this conversation with lots of parents. I do understand it's hard to let go."

No, you don't understand at all.

Crushed, I went home, feeling like a complete failure. I was banned from the playground! Forbidden from entering my daughter's school! The shame was like quicksand, and I sank deeper and deeper. This was all my own fault. I was to blame. I was ruining my children's lives now, as well as my own. My overprotectiveness had backfired spectacularly. In trying so hard to look after my children, I was in fact failing them. I desperately wanted to change. I wished, more than anything, I could erase the memories of my own childhood. But I just didn't know how.

At parents' evenings, I was way out of my depth. I felt the disapproval crackling as the teachers passed silent, tight-lipped, judgement on me as a mother.

"Lucy doesn't always have her reading book," they said. "And could you make sure she brings in £5 for art club? And can you try and send her in on time?"

Each comment felt like a direct assault. Each criticism was confirmation that I was no good as a parent. And I was disorganised, certainly. I had no role model, no idea at all, of how a normal childhood should be. I was a complete stranger to concepts such as homework and school plays and spelling tests. I embraced all of this, as I encountered it, and I did my best. But I punished myself mercilessly for my mistakes.

"Just get her to school on time," I muttered to myself. "How hard can it be?"

And though I was keen for my children to make friends, I could not give permission for them to go on playdates or sleepovers. Even as Lucy grew older, I did not allow her to play outside.

"Let's invite your pals round to our house instead," I suggested.

The irony was, I was only just about capable of looking after myself and my children, never mind anyone else's kids. But the need for me to keep my children close was not superficial nor was it negotiable. I didn't necessarily see it as the best option, but for me, this was the only option. It was a primeval, visceral instinct. Like a mother lion, gently nudging her cubs back to the den, I had to keep my babies close by.

* * * *

Even now, when I was solely responsible for my own home, I could not bring myself to use a front door key. Deep down, I just did not believe I deserved it. I had spent so many years longing for a home of my own, a family, a front door, and a set of keys. For a place I felt loved and welcome. Now, I was so scared of admitting I was putting down roots, always wary of everything I held dear being ripped away from me. It bordered on superstitious; I thought by becoming complacent, I was asking for trouble.

In most of my flats, I'd been on the first or second floor, and so I'd simply leave the front door on the latch, so I could easily get back inside. But now, I had a ground floor flat, which opened out onto a busy street, and I was apprehensive about leaving the door unlocked. Instead, I went out each day, letting the latch fall automatically behind me. When I returned, I climbed in through a back window, which had a loose catch. It was an arrangement which worked perfectly well for me, and I didn't even view it as particularly unusual. But after a few months, I had a visit from a social worker.

"I'll be straight with you," she said. "We've had a report from one of your neighbours that you've been seen climbing in and out of the windows. They seem to think you might be putting the children at risk. Are they in the house on their own?"

I groaned heavily.

"No," I replied. "Absolutely not."

Cringing, I explained my routine of letting the front door lock, and then later letting myself in through the window.

"The children are outside with me," I explained. "We climb through the window together. At no point have I ever left them on their own or put them at any risk."

The social worker nodded.

"That's good enough for me," she said. "But why don't you just use your keys?"

My eyes swam with humiliated tears.

"I can't cope with keys," I said quietly. "I'm sorry."

The social worker offered me support and this time, knowing I had to move forwards, I accepted. I signed up for a positive parenting course, where I learned how to get into a better routine with the children and manage difficult behaviour. Lucy was like a little doll; she was cute and beautiful, and she followed me like a shadow. Jake was boisterous, diving off furniture, racing around the flat at full speed. He'd be kicking a football under the dining table at mealtimes or racing his cars whilst he was supposed to be getting dressed for school. They were both so completely different; both so completely perfect. For my part, I wanted to be the best parent I could.

On the advice of the social worker, I also made an appointment with Citizens Advice, to help manage my money. One of my goals was to get off benefits, and as soon as the children were old enough, I was determined to return to work and be more self-sufficient. But as I arrived at the offices, I saw a poster in the window, asking for volunteers. Jake was soon to start at nursery and so the timing was ideal. On the spur of the moment, I said:

"I saw your notice; please would you consider me? I'd really like to help out."

I was delighted when they agreed. My first few shifts were spent photocopying and making cups of tea. I got the distinct impression they were scratching around to find tasks for me; they were as keen to help me as I was them. Within a few months, I was offered a training course, to become a caseworker, helping people to find housing. I went from voluntary to paid work and found myself working with families similar to my own, supporting children in bedsits and homeless accommodation. It was like digging into my own past, and yet this time, there was a positive outcome.

As well as offering hope to other families, I was helping to heal myself. In time, I was promoted again, and I started working within prisons, helping prisoners and their families to access the support they needed. At work, I was excelling. My career was taking off. I was off benefits, I was earning well, and I success-fully juggled life as a mother and as a respected professional. My children were well-cared for and well-loved. At weekends, I'd pack us a picnic and, weather depending, take a towel or wellington boots down to the local park, where there was a paddling pool. Sometimes we'd spend the whole day there.

In summer, we went to Butlins and there were days out to the seaside and to funfairs. Lucy enrolled at a local dance school, and we went together to buy her first pair of sparkly dance shoes. I beamed as the assistant wrapped them in tissue paper and I handed over the money.

"This was what real mothers do," I told myself. "You're getting it right, at last."

Jake was football mad, and I spent my Saturday mornings shivering on the touchline, watching him play for a local team. He was covered head to foot in mud most weekends. But I wouldn't have had it any other way. I was so grateful for all of these small gems which added up to make me into a mother. And yet, the bogeyman was still there, like a squatter in my brain, dragging me down, reminding me just who I was and where I had come from. I felt like a fraud, each morning at work, and again each evening with the children.

At dance class, I never once spoke with the other parents; I just didn't feel I was good enough. They seemed to sneer at me as I took my seat to watch the shows. Perhaps they did push me out, or maybe, I did it all by myself. I felt strongly I did not deserve all the happiness and success which was coming my way. And so, over and over again, I sought solace in wine. I was a workaholic. I was also an alcoholic. All my adult life, I had expected this challenge; I ticked both the nature and nurture boxes after all. But I had not factored in how momentous the test would be, smothering me like a blanket and dominating my thoughts.

I am not like her, I am not.

You are exactly like her. You are.

Those accusations were so unbearable, I had to drink even more to escape them. The irony was so cruel. The parallels with my mother were glaring, but I would not, could not, see them.

38

JUST LIKE any new mother, I instinctively wanted to share the joy of my children with my wider family. No matter how my parents had failed me, I owed it to everyone involved to give them an opportunity to make amends through Lucy and Jake. When I made contact, they were living in the same house in Hackney, in the same chaos.

"I have two rules," I told them. "You must not drink around my children, and I don't want any punters around either."

I had low expectations for our first meeting, but I was pleasantly surprised. My parents, both sober, were overjoyed to meet Lucy and Jake. They had a bag of presents waiting, and my dad insisted on taking Lucy to Woolworths to buy a toy.

"All above board, no thieving," my dad told me, waving a 10-pound note in the air.

For a while, the arrangement seemed to work well. I visited two or three times a year, making a conscious effort to ignore past demons and concentrate only on the present. But, like anything with my mother and father, it could not last. During one visit, I heard a familiar voice in the kitchen and, when I popped my head around the door, my stomach turned.

"Albert," I gasped.

"He's just a family friend," Dad insisted. "What's the problem?"

But in that moment, I was six years old again, cowering in the wet bed, feeling the cold of the coin in my palm. To my surprise, he was not the city hot-shot my childish imagination had built him up to be. In late middle-age, he was still unmarried, living with his mother, a weak and inadequate man. I remembered the briefcase he used to carry, his symbol of success, and I almost laughed. It was pitiful. I looked from him to my mother, who was gulping whiskey from a coffee mug. I said nothing but turned on my heel, took the children, and left.

For weeks afterwards, I was furious. I had given them one chance and they had blown it, breaking both my rules at once. Despite myself, I was disappointed, not for me, but for the kids. Yet as time went on, my anger softened into an enduring sadness. As an adult, I realised for the first time, how miserable their lives were, because of addiction. But there was to be no going back. My already hardened heart calcified further against them, and the contact ended that day.

For different reasons, it was also difficult to maintain relationships with my three brothers. Spending time together only seemed to trigger memories of the past and it didn't help that physically I looked very similar to our mother. Sometimes, just the sight of me was enough to send them spiralling back to a childhood they were trying to forget.

In 2002, I got a call to say Dad had passed away. He'd had a drunken fall, and later, in hospital, had suffered a stroke. In the end, alcohol had finished him, just as I always feared it would. His funeral, at a London crematorium, was attended only by me, my brothers, my mother and – I noticed him with a shudder – Albert. I was horrified to hear Albert had paid for the funeral, and also for the catering afterwards. It was mind-bogglingly strange and, in my opinion, deeply inappropriate and offensive.

"Come back to the house," Mum said. "Please."

"No thanks," I said shortly. "I came to say goodbye to my dad, and that was all."

"Please," she said again, more softly this time and I felt a stab of guilt. It seemed cruel, leaving her alone, today of all days. But when I arrived at our old family home, I heard the familiar chink of bottles in a carrier bag, and I spotted Albert, lurking in the hallway. Without even taking off my coat, I made my excuses and left. There was no court order to force me back in there. No adults telling me what to do. I was in charge of myself. The knowledge was empowering and despite the sadness of the funeral, I felt a sense of peace as I drove away.

* * * *

Lucy and Jake did well through primary school, and though each milestone was blemished by my own trauma, I was immensely proud and happy. Each year, before their birthdays, I handed them an Argos catalogue.

"Draw a circle around everything you like," I told them.

Even though I was working full-time, I took loans out, twice a year, for their birthdays and Christmas. I went all out to over-compensate. Remembering my own birthdays, some of which passed by completely unmarked, worse still others which ended in fights and misery, made me so sad. I was determined my own children should know nothing of my suffering. Christmas, too, was an overblown affair, with too many presents and too much food. But I always told myself, you could never have too much love.

Secretly, I hated Christmas. For many years, it had been a cruel reminder of what was missing in my life. For my parents, the festive season was a lazy excuse to get even more drunk than usual and smash the place up. Christmas represented only broken furniture and broken dreams. But I was careful never to let the children know my true feelings and I learned to celebrate traditionally, just like any other family. I was intent on cutting my emotional ties to the past, just as surely as if I'd taken a giant pair of scissors and snipped right through the link.

In addition to overdoing it at celebrations, I went overboard with cleanliness too. The memory of being a smelly kid haunted me, just like the smell itself, and I was adamant my own children should never experience the shame and sheer humiliation of poor hygiene. Right from the moment they were born, I washed and rewashed their clothes in the best fabric softener, and even though I was often short of money when they were little, I always over-spent on washing products. For me, cleanliness was a non-negotiable necessity. I scrubbed and polished each rented home we had, until it gleamed and shone. I wanted a place they could be proud of. And a mother they could be proud of too.

Whilst the children were indulged on occasion, I was mostly very strict. I raised them to have impeccable manners and good behaviour, and they were not allowed to shout or swear in the family home. They would have been horrified to hear my own colourful language, at their age. As they grew older, they were not allowed to stay out late or drink alcohol under-age, and I warned them daily against the scourge of drugs. Once, I even printed off a picture of a woman whose face had been ravaged by a crystal meth addiction. I pinned the images to the fridge and told them:

"This is what will happen to you if you take drugs! All your teeth will fall out, just like hers!"

The hypocrisy of my warnings rang loudly in my ears; I had stumbled through my own childhood in a haze of alcohol, aerosol gas and cannabis. I had ongoing addictions as an adult to booze and food. But being a mother, for me, was about breaking that cycle. It was about not repeating the mistakes of my own parents, and grandparents, and who knows how many generations before them. I was determined not to use my own background as an excuse for parenting weaknesses. And as a result, I was definitely more rigid and strait-laced than other parents.

After those first few bumpy years at school, I made education a priority. I insisted homework was done and teachers were given the respect they deserved. Lucy, like me, was an avid little reader and learner, and that gave me great joy. My own lack of education had impacted right through my life, not only in terms of qualifications, but also, and more importantly, in the limits I placed upon myself. As a little girl my life's goals had been not to end up like my mother, and not to be a sex worker. As I grew older, they were modified into not being evicted and not living on benefits. Everything I had wished for, I realised sadly, was a negative. That in itself spoke volumes. My own children had fantastically vaulting ambitions.

"When I grow up, I want to travel the world and work in construction," Jake told me.

"And when I grow up, I want to go to university," Lucy said.

Hearing the width and breadth of their hopes and dreams made my heart sing. Perhaps I had got something right after all.

39

ONE WARM evening in the summer of 2005, the children had been playing out with their friends. I had been working hard on my paranoia to allow them some freedom outside our home; Lucy, now aged 12, was allowed to play at the park at the bottom of our street. Jake, now nine, was allowed to play just outside the house, with a friend. I felt like I stopped breathing each time they left the house, but I was making slow progress. Before dark, they were both home and got ready for bed. I opened a bottle of wine downstairs and had soon polished it off. The kids were sound asleep by the time I'd finished the second bottle, and I followed that up with a couple of Bacardis. As I lay on the sofa, with the room spinning violently, the doorbell rang. It was after 9pm and I was far too drunk to answer the door, but I staggered into the hallway regardless. I almost collapsed when I saw a police community support officer standing in the porch.

"Sorry it's so late," he said. "It's nothing to worry about. There was an incident earlier outside the park, where the kids were messing about by the edge of the road. Your daughter was one of them and it could have been dangerous. So I took their names and I'm speaking to all the parents. Just a reminder of road safety."

I leaned against the doorframe, barely able to focus on his face.

"Shorry," I slurred.

It was all I could manage. At some point, I closed the door, possibly whilst he was still speaking. Slumping onto the hallway carpet, I felt my whole body trembling. Drunk as I was, I was fully aware I'd just opened the door to a PCSO, and I was completely incapable of speech. In just a few seconds, I sobered up, as though an invisible hoover was sucking all the alcohol from my body. Panic spread through me like a rash.

"You've blown it now," I told myself. "You absolute fool. He's bound to report you. Social services will definitely come for the kids. All your fault. Again."

With my head in my hands, I cried. I didn't know what to do. I felt sure he would make a referral, to the children's school and to social services. How could I possibly explain being so paralytically smashed, when I was in charge of two children? The issue of Lucy misbehaving at the park passed me by, unnoticed. I had far bigger worries on my mind.

By the next morning, I had reached a decision. I needed help. Real help. I knew the number for the local rehab centre; I was used to referring clients there at work. I knew all the staff. And so it was especially humbling and embarrassing for me to have to phone and admit I had a problem myself.

"I'm falling apart," I admitted. "Please help me."

The children thought I was going away to work, but instead I went into residential detox. They stayed with a good friend for two weeks. When I was discharged, I was sober, and determined to stay that way. I'd had time off work, and decided perhaps I needed a new direction, where there were none of my previous associations and triggers for alcohol. Instead of returning to my old job, I helped set up a homeless shelter in Southampton. I began doing voluntary work in night shelters and with women's charities.

In 2014 I wrote and published a book, called *Hackney Child*, which told the story of my early years. The response to the book was overwhelmingly positive, and I was invited to speak both to kids in care, and to care providers. In time, I was offered a role by the local authority, delivering keynote speeches and training programmes to social workers, police officers, teachers and youth workers. I was even awarded an honorary doctorate, after working with students at the University of Huddersfield. I was also made patron of Trevi, a charity supporting women and children affected by abuse.

Along the way, I bumped into many old faces from the past. At a Fostering Panel, I found myself sitting next to a social worker whose name I recognised as the same one who had closed the door on the possibility of me being fostered, aged 14. She had no memory of me, and why would she? I was merely one child amongst thousands, and she had no inkling of the catastrophic impact of that decision; like so many of the decisions made on behalf of kids in care. I worked with professionals who knew Dot and Jeff, and Marj and Brian. I tried to track down Lara, but discovered she had struggled after leaving care, and tragically died from an overdose. Even though I hadn't seen her since we were teenagers, I felt a chasm of loss inside. She'd been my first best friend, my only best friend, really. My mind went back to Lara playing the guitar, belting out heavy metal, laughing at my homemade tattoo, covering for me when I was late back at the children's home. She'd been full of life, bursting with promise, until it was drained out of her by the care system. Until there was not a drop left.

One day, we'll get our own place, and we can do as we like.

"Miss you, Lara," I whispered.

I traced the other girls from the children's home, even the bullies. We were all on the same side now, maybe we had been all along. One afternoon, I was stuck in gridlocked traffic when I saw a new email pop up on my phone. As I glanced at the subject line, my insides did a somersault.

'Aerobics instructor/firefighter.'

With shaking hands, I pulled over to the side of the road and clicked to open. It could only be from one person – but how?

"I saw you in the newspaper, when your book came out," Debbie wrote. "We are the people who wanted to foster you, Hope. I wondered if you would like to meet?"

My heart was racing. Here it was, 30 years too late, an email from my foster mother. I remembered how much I had longed to hear from her, and my heart ached. I arranged to go and see her and Darren later that week, but as the day came around, my excitement was displaced by a creeping sense of dread. I was opening a locked box, a portal to the past, and I wasn't sure I was up to the task. Yet Debbie and Daz were, in every way, just as I had dreamed. Warm, kind, loving. Debbie showed me the bedroom I would, should, have had.

"We had everything ready for you," she said sadly. "But you never came."

She and Daz had never fostered. They had waited years for news of what had happened to me – what exactly went wrong remains a mystery – and they never got an answer. Badly hurt, they hadn't reapplied. The meeting sent me hurtling back into my childhood and for weeks afterwards, I wasn't sure I could bear to see them again. The wounds were raw and painful, and, in many ways, it felt futile, dredging over past mistakes, and finding out what could have been. Eventually, one step at a time, Debbie and I built up a relationship, and I realised we could be friends, looking forwards and not back.

At around the same time, I was reunited with my teacher, Marie. She invited me to speak at her school, where she was now headteacher. Afterwards, we stayed in touch, and I loved receiving her letters. They were always a boost.

"You were always 'My Hope,'" she wrote. "Not knowing what had happened to you was really hard. I love that your spirit is still there and that you are still fighting for the child in you and in others. You are an inspiration."

Her words brought me to tears. I'd had no idea I'd had such an impact on any of these people. I'd thought the influence was all one way. Perhaps I wasn't quite so worthless, after all.

40

THE FOLLOWING year, I was invited to speak at a conference in Hartlepool, addressing representatives from the police, social services, health and education. I'd been asked to talk about being a child in care. And though I could recount every detail, sharp as flint, in my memory, the prospect terrified me. These, after all, were the same agencies who'd been responsible for my upbringing. Now I was here to advise them. It just didn't seem right.

I began my speech as planned but inexplicably, I suddenly heard myself talking about Dougie.

"When I was a teenager, I was numb to relationships," I told them. "In fact, at 14, I had an affair with an older man, my friend's husband actually."

My heart hammering, I wanted to grab the words and swallow them back down. But it was too late. I couldn't believe I'd confessed to a room full of strangers. What was I thinking? I couldn't wait to get out of there.

As I finished my speech and stepped down from the podium, a young, dark haired police officer came over.

"Can I ask you something?" he said. "You mentioned your affair with an older man?"

"Yeah," I muttered. "I was a little slag back then, I do apologise."

It was crass. Painfully embarrassing. But truly, it was what I believed.

"No," he said firmly. "No. It wasn't an affair. It was child abuse. Have you heard of CSE?"

I shook my head.

"Child Sexual Exploitation," he said. "You were the victim. Not the perpetrator. There was no affair, Hope. There was no relationship."

I was shell-shocked.

"Are you sure? Nobody has ever told me this before. It was my fault, I'm sure it was. I knew he was married, and I just went ahead anyway."

Even now, years on, my face burned with shame.

"It absolutely was not your fault," he assured me. "Nowadays, he'd be arrested, and you'd be taken to a place of safety. I'm only sorry you didn't get the support you needed."

* * * *

Despite the assurances of the police officer, I could not bring myself to report Dougie. I didn't have the vocabulary or the understanding, still, of what had happened to me. And it was buried, so deeply, I was not sure I would ever be able to retrieve it. All my adult life, I'd been frightened that Dougie would come after me. It had never once occurred to me that I might go after him.

As the days went by, I convinced myself the police officer was in fact well-meaning but a little naïve. How on earth could I go to the police, now, after all this time? I wasn't even sure a crime had been committed, and it was over 30 years ago too. They'd laugh me out of the police station no doubt. I vowed to repackage the whole thing back into the depths of my consciousness. And yet, it wasn't so easy. Like prodding a nest of ants, my conversation with the police officer had awakened all my old fears and misgivings.

One night, on my laptop, I came across The Truth Project, an independent inquiry into Child Sexual Abuse. The website explained it offered a safe and supportive opportunity for victims and survivors to share their story. The form was online and so, for the first time, I wrote down everything that had happened to me in the care system, starting aged nine, ending aged 18. It was part confessional, part cathartic, scribbling down everything I could remember, details and facts which I'd never dreamed I'd share with another human being. By the end of it, I was wiped out. I had hoped this emotional purging might relieve me of some of the memories; instead they only grew more vivid. There were echoes everywhere; a four-pack of super-strength lager in the supermarket, the smell of cannabis as I walked through the city, I even saw a young girl wearing purple dungarees one day and the image choked me. One day, I found myself driving for over an hour, back to where I thought Dougie had lived, searching for a red phone box outside a high-rise block of flats. When I arrived at the area, I was greeted by a new housing estate. No phone box. No flats. No Dougie. Confused, I parked my car and got out. Was this even the right place? The pavements seemed different. The old shops had gone. The new houses stared at me, mocking and smug.

Are you sure this ever happened? We all know what you're like, you girls from care. Terrible liars.

In tears, I got back in the car once again. Perhaps his block had been knocked down. I wasn't sure I'd found the right street. But I was certain of one thing: I could not continue battling this nightmare. I would have to flush it out and face it head on, once and for all. The next day, trembling with anticipation, I called the police. An appointment was made for me to see a historical abuse officer at a London police station. Just walking in was a challenge; the last time I'd been in a station was as a runaway teenager, escaping from a secure unit, or a children's home, or from Dougie. I couldn't shake the feeling, even now, that I was in the wrong.

"I'm really sorry," the officer said. "All our rooms are full. We'll have to do the interview in one of these glass booths."

I stared at her in disbelief. The poky booths in front of us were separated by flimsy looking perspex. There was no sound proofing at all. It was completely exposed.

"I can't talk to you in here," I stuttered, my voice no more than a whisper. "I'm reporting sexual offences."

She looked at me as if to say I had no other option. In the end, I gave a very brief account of what had happened, conscious that everyone around us could hear me too.

"We'll be in touch," she promised.

Again, I tried to push it out of my mind. Again, it was impossible. I kept myself busy with work and I enrolled at Open University, alongside Lucy. When the police got in touch, it was to say they had lost my statement, and I was required to make another. In all, I made three statements. Gradually the wall around me was being knocked down, brick by brick. But picking away at the cement, shaking the structure which had imprisoned me for so long, filled me with fear. I just wasn't sure I could do this. It was beginning to feel more and more impossible. Besides, I didn't know Dougie's surname, or his age, or his address. Then, the officers realised the case spanned four separate police forces.

"We need you to speak to other officers, from other forces, to try and pull all this together," I was told.

I gave four different video interviews, one after the other. It was draining. I felt like a dishcloth, squeezed dry. Incredibly, through social media, we were able to track Dougie down and he was arrested.

"He admits having sex, he admits meeting you in the woods and the derelict house, everything just as you describe," the officer said.

I allowed my heart to rise a little, in hope.

"But he insists he thought you were 16 years old, and it was a consensual relationship, and we have no way of proving him wrong," he finished.

My heart plummeted.

"How could I be 16 and still in a children's home?" I protested. "He's lying. You know he's lying."

"I am really sorry," the officer said. "But we don't have enough evidence for it to go to court."

It was not, strangely, as devastating or as shocking as I might have expected. There was even an element of relief that I would not have to face the court process. All along, I had thought the police would dismiss me out of hand. The fact that they had believed me and taken me seriously was vital. I had a voice. I had worth. I was no longer the little slut, the little slag, the little whore.

41

AN OVERSPILL from the police investigation was that I began to examine more broadly my previous understanding of sexual violence against women. It was impossible not to consider my own mother in this. I questioned my previous attitude of Dad as blameless, and Mum as perpetrator. As a mother myself, I was more critical of her, but I was also more sympathetic towards her. I got her address from one of my brothers and wrote. I'd had no contact at all with her since the day I caught her drinking when the children were small, and so when there was no reply, I was not surprised. I was not sure the address was up to date, or if she was even still alive. My big worry was that, as an alcoholic, she would die and have a pauper's funeral. I wanted to at least take care of that for her. The days passed, still I didn't hear back. I told myself it didn't matter; I hadn't seen her for 20 years anyway. And yet I couldn't deny a small pang of disappointment. Over a week later, my phone rang. I'd have known that voice anywhere.

"I'm really sorry, I've been on holiday," she said. "I've just this minute opened your letter. I want you to know I'm sober. I'd love to see you and the kids, I really would."

"I'll come," I promised.

I arranged to visit her, that weekend, at her home in Kent. Preparing myself for the usual chaos, I was stunned when Mum answered the door to a neat and tidy flat. There was no smell, no mess, no noise.

"Is this where you live?" I asked, stunned.

I was more taken aback by the transformation in Mum's living accommodation than I was by the changes in her. And yet, as I took my seat on a clean and comfortable sofa, I noticed too how well she was looking. She was glamorous, even as a pensioner. Her hair was dyed, and her make-up was perfect. She was older and frailer certainly. But she was still in heels, just not quite as high. And her lipstick was as red as ever.

"I've been sober for over 10 years," she told me proudly. "And I feel so much better for it."

In many ways, she was still unmistakably herself; forceful, resilient, independent. Yet without the addiction, she was also funny and kind, thoughtful and affectionate. I came away from her home with my head buzzing. I was pleased she had beaten her demons, but filled with sadness for what might have been. It was too late for my childhood. We would never have a mother and daughter relationship, but I hoped we could at least be friends. Most of all, I hoped she could be a grandmother to Lucy and Jake. I took them to see her, and she was an instant hit.

"I've missed out on so many years," Mum told me. "I want to make up for as much as I can."

Over the months, we became close; closer without doubt than we had ever been. Alcohol addiction had blurred her memories of the past, but despite everything, I warmed to her.

"I lost six kids," she told me sadly. "You can't begin to imagine how sorry I am."

Mum told me she'd been taken into care as a child, and, after persistently absconding, she was placed in a secure unit. Amazingly, I had been in the very same unit myself, aged 13.

"Like mother, like daughter," Mum laughed ruefully.

It was a comparison which once would have infuriated me but now, I didn't mind it so much. Her life had mirrored my own in some ways and, for the first time, I appreciated how hard it had been for her. On one occasion, running away, she'd jumped out of the bathroom window at the unit and shattered her ankle.

"It still gives me pain now," she admitted, showing me the bump on the bone.

Aged 15, she was raped by an older man but was too ashamed to tell anyone. Just as I had, she blamed herself, another echo from own childhood. At 16, she became pregnant by a married man who she met through her part-time job at a cinema. She gave birth to a baby girl, named Sylvia, but was immediately told she could not keep her.

"I took the baby to my boyfriend's house," Mum said sadly. "I figured if he saw her, just once, he'd want her. She had fair hair like him, she looked like him, and I thought he'd love her. But he didn't. He turned us away and I cried all the way back, on the Underground. I didn't even have a baby blanket, I had to cover her with my coat."

Sylvia was placed for adoption and Mum later met Dad, who was much older than her and already an alcoholic. He too had been through the care system, having been dumped as a baby at the doors of an orphanage. He didn't even have a date of birth. Life with Dad was chaotic from the start, and they lived in furnished rooms and hostels.

"I loved your dad, but he was a way out for me," Mum confessed.

She fell pregnant again and had a second daughter, Jacqueline. With no home, and no money, she was persuaded to give the baby to a family who could look after her properly. For the next 10 years, she and Dad had no more children.

"I thought it was a punishment," Mum said. "I'd given away two babies, so this was God's way of telling me I didn't deserve another. And I didn't."

But in her late twenties, Mum eventually had my eldest brother, Philip. One night soon after, Dad was out drinking, and she had no money for baby milk or for heating. It was in these lonely, desperate circumstances that Mum made what many would view as an appalling mistake. Others, though, would say she was incredibly brave.

"There was a lorry park nearby," she told me, without emotion. "I went out, knocked on a cab, and asked if he wanted sex."

So that was how it had started. My mother became a prostitute to feed her children. It could arguably be seen as the ultimate sacrifice, the greatest display of maternal devotion. She slept with strangers, night after night, as a way of providing for her family. Much as I loathed what she did, I felt an unexpected sense of admiration too. In the meantime, she and Dad moved from one place to another, leaving hurriedly each time they fell behind with the rent or rowed with the neighbours. Once, Dad emptied the gas meter and they had to flee in the middle of the night. When Mum finally confessed that she was selling herself, she expected, hoped maybe, that Dad would be furious and ban her from ever doing it again. Instead, he endorsed it. He spotted an income stream and grasped it with both hands. By the time I was born, Mum was also an addict, and she had a steady supply of regulars coming to the house, which at least meant she no longer had to walk the streets. But her earnings now went on alcohol, and not on her children. Over the years, she'd been in prison several times for soliciting, and dad was convicted twice of living off immoral earnings. He was also jailed for shoplifting. Mum stood by him and though she wanted to leave him, she also loved him in her own way.

The night before I was taken into care, when our family home was smashed up, a neighbour had discovered her own husband was one of Mum's clients. She organised a lynch mob to smash up our home and drive us out. As was always the way – and perhaps it still is – Mum, and not the woman's husband, was targeted. It is generally expected that women should know better. Society puts a greater pressure on mothers and on wives.

"When I was released from prison, you were all gone," Mum told me. "I had nothing left. Your dad was there, surrounded by all the mess, drunk as a lord."

Mum was a prostitute for 40 years, giving it up only after my father died. By now, she was in her early 60s. After turning 70, she suddenly made the decision to give up drinking and had not once relapsed.

Her story, seen through the softer lens of motherhood, broke my heart. I couldn't decide where the blame lay, and if it was indeed too simplistic to apportion blame. My parents had suffered immeasurably as children. But that did not excuse the way they had failed their own children. Growing up, I had laid most of the responsibility on my mother. I expected better of her. And yet now I could see she had been controlled and coerced by my father. She had been subject to serious sexual assault and had suffered the loss of two of her daughters. My own life had been tough, but hers was tragic.

When I had my own children, I was so focused on breaking the cycle of abuse that I looked only forwards. I could not look backwards at the same time. When I dared to look back, I saw that Mum was not the start of the problems. She was not the monster I had built her up to be. She was simply another link in the chain.

I had grown up not wanting to be like my mother, but I could see now that she did not want to be like her either. And, in some small ways, I was proud of the similarities. Her strength and resilience had kept her going, all these years. She had spent much of her life alone, but she was the very definition of a survivor. Slowly, I learned acceptance, on my terms. I had to forgive her, to find peace myself and for my own children. And for her sake too. Like a seedling, pushing tentatively through the earth, my redemptive love for my mother germinated and grew.

42

THROUGHOUT THE police investigation, I had been sorely tempted, more than once, to turn to alcohol. My thoughts streamed in all directions, like water running over stones, and I could not collect them together. Sometimes, my head was so noisy and so busy, and I longed for a few moments of calm. I was determined I would not drink, and instead, I sought solace in eating. My relationship with food had always been fraught. Though I didn't recognise it, I had an eating disorder, and chocolate was as much an addiction as alcohol. By 2020, I tipped the scales at over 17 stone, and even then, I purged many of the calories through vomiting. I had tried various diets, over the years, but they simply scratched at the top layer of a problem which felt bottomless. And so, plucking up my courage, I saw my GP and pleaded to be referred for private bariatric surgery. At a cost of £10 000, it didn't come cheap, but I was working full-time and earning well. By now, Lucy and I had also graduated with degrees in youth justice; a realisation of a dream for us both.

Early in 2021, I had gastric sleeve surgery at a Harley Street clinic, which was a success. In the months which followed, I lost over seven stone. Critically, my operation forced me to address my relationship with food. I had been warned the chances of me relapsing as an alcoholic, post-surgery, were high, and I was on my guard against temptation. But when the bait was laid it was from such a shocking source that I was completely unprepared.

I was awarded £38,000 as part of the Lambeth Redress scheme, which paid compensation to people who were abused in care as children. This covered my time in the secure units. I was not awarded compensation from the authorities in Hackney, in relation to my early years, nor was I compensated for the sexual grooming and rapes by Dougie, and the trauma in foster care, from different areas around the country. I was told many social services records, including my own, had been destroyed in a cyber-attack.

One evening, with time on my hands, and not wishing to be tempted either by food or drink, I went to the local casino. I had never in my life been inside a casino and my decision was as weird as it was reckless. It was like being 15 again, with my legs running towards Dougie, whilst my brain screamed out against it. That first night, I lost and won back the same £500 many times and by the time I left, I was addicted. Gambling, like alcohol, like sugar rushes, gave me a chance to lose myself for a while. I didn't care how much it cost. For me, the feeling was priceless. But very quickly, I was out of my depth. I might call in at the casino after work, telling myself I'd spend maybe an hour there. Yet I'd still be slumped over a table at 4am the next morning. I burned through my compensation in under six months. Staring at my bank statements, I realised, with a slurry of dismay, that I had a serious problem. The next day, a Monday, I spoke with the manager of the casino and asked him to admit me only at weekends.

"I need to cut down on my spending," I explained.

I drove home, happily deluded that I had at least tried to address the problem. But as the day wore on, I heard the roulette tables whispering my name. I felt a magnetic pull towards the slot machines. There was a second casino, a little further away, and so I spoke to the manager there, and asked him only to allow me in on weekdays. It was a ludicrous arrangement, where I was blatantly conning myself. At the time, I thought I was taking sensible steps to limit my gambling. Looking back now, I can see this was another dangerous slip, on an inevitable downward spiral.

Christmas 2021 was harder than usual. For the sake of the kids, by now grown up with little ones of their own, I put on a show. After we had opened our gifts and eaten an early dinner, I made my excuses to attend a celebration for care leavers. I remembered only too well the desolation and loneliness of my teenage years, and so, with the support of a local charity, I'd helped organise a Christmas Day party. Watching them all arrive, with their all-knowing smiles and heavy make-up, yawning with hangovers and disinterest, they didn't fool me one bit. Underneath the façade, they were still little boys and girls. I was busy cello-taping layers onto a pass-the-parcel, when another volunteer said to me:

"Don't you think they're too young for party games? Pass the Parcel is for little kids really."

"They've never had the chance to be little kids," I replied. "Trust me, they will love it."

Later, my eyes filled with tears as they giggled and squabbled each time the music stopped. I watched as they clutched the parcel, in the same way they must have gripped desperately onto childhood as it was snatched from them. Oh, I recognised that anguish. Afterwards, the discarded sheets of newspaper, ripped to shreds, spoke volumes. That night, when I was back home, Lucy called.

"How did the party go?" she asked. "What a way to spend Christmas Day, Mum, giving your day up for other people."

"Oh that was the easy part," I replied. "Going home was the worst. None of them wanted to leave, back to their hostels and their little flats. I know how lonely that is and it broke my heart."

43

INTO 2022, my gambling addiction, still a closely guarded secret, was ravaging my finances. I was plagued more and more
by reminders of my teenage years. The police investigation,
and subsequent psychiatric assessments before the award of
compensation, had brought all the memories right to the fore-
front of my mind. I was persecuted by ghouls from the past.
Once uncorked, this brewing panic would not go back obediently into the bottle. I was not sleeping or eating properly, and
at work, I was smothering panic attacks and palpitations, like I
was putting fires out everywhere. Again, just as in my teens, I
became hyper-critical of myself.

*How can you, of all people, lecture professionals on how to look after
kids? You can't even look after yourself! You were right all along. You're a
little slut, a little whore, a little slag. You're a joke.*

I had a prescription for strong painkillers, for fibromyalgia,
and in desperation I began popping one or two each evening.
But still, my heart raced. My mind was like a three-lane
motorway, with vehicles whizzing past at top speed. A pile-up
was inevitable. In many ways, I wanted to crash. I wanted it all
to be over. Pressing my foot on the accelerator, I saw driving
into a brick wall as my only option. So when the painkillers ran

low, I started alternating them with a glass of wine. Alcohol one night. Tablets the next.

You're an alcoholic. You've relapsed. You need help.

But I had never liked listening to the sensible voice, not then, and not now.

Chill out. It's just a glass of wine. You can cope with that.

Soon though, I was drinking heavily every night. At work, I kept up some sort of patchy routine, though I imagine people around me had guessed I was beginning to sink. My job kept me going, but it was also in part, the problem. Addressing issues of child sexual exploitation and neglect every day was rewarding. But it was wounding, nonetheless. Socially, I cut myself off completely. I called Lucy and Jake every day, but that was as far as my interaction went. I was slipping and sliding, without a foothold to keep me steady. The year wore on, and with Christmas in sight, I was struck with what I thought was a flash of absolute brilliance. Quite randomly, I stumbled across the perfect solution to all my problems: I would kill myself.

"Christmas is coming, death is coming," I told myself.

It was such an obvious remedy; my only surprise was I had not thought of this before. I began making meticulous plans. I made a will, I wrote letters to my children and grandchildren, and I left details and passwords for my bank accounts and my domestic admin. Lastly, with a growing sense of excitement and anticipation, I scrubbed my flat until it shone. With everything in order, I had just one job left to do. I did not have a specific date in mind, except that it must be done before December 31. On Christmas Eve, I went out to buy Prosecco, to accompany my overdose. But as I stood in the supermarket, I felt a spontaneous surge of extravagance. Grabbing a bottle of Champagne, I paid at the till with a smile on my face.

Might as well go out in style.

On December 27, at 7.20pm, I poured myself a glass of ice-cold Moet and emptied the first lot of pills out onto the coffee table. I felt perfectly at peace, and saner than I had ever been.

I sent my colleague an email with the letters to my children and a spreadsheet of my passwords to help them sort my affairs out after I had died. The subject line said: 'Things to tie up after my death'. I was certain she wouldn't see the email until January 4, when the offices reopened, and by then, I'd be long gone. Rereading the email briefly, I was pleased with the tone. It was efficient and unsentimental, with no suggestion of crisis or urgency. Back at the coffee table, swallowing more pills, I finished off the Moet and lay down to sleep.

* * * *

When I woke up, I was, firstly, confused to be awake at all.

"Why am I not dead?" I yelled. "Why?"

Lucy and Jake, at my bedside, patiently explained that my colleague, in a complete fluke, had logged into her work emails later on the evening of December 27. I was unconscious when paramedics found me, and I'd been in a coma for four days in hospital. For a further two days, I was locked in a deep psychosis. Lucy lay on my bed, holding my hand, stroking my face, and caring for me. It breaks my heart, as I look back, how worried she and Jake must have been. But at the time, I was trapped in my own private version of hell.

The psychiatric unit, where I was a patient, looked and smelled exactly like the secure units of my teenage years and, in my bewilderment, I believed I had somehow teleported back to 1987. The bed, with the same sterile standard issue blue mattress, was nailed to the floor. There was a hatch in the door which was snapped open hourly. The walls, floors and ceiling were the same neutral porridge colour. I couldn't tell where the floor finished, and where the ceiling began. The monotony made me want to scream. When I was well enough to sit up, I grabbed my duvet and went to sleep in the communal living room.

"I'm not going back in the bedroom," I said darkly. "Not ever."

"You don't need to be afraid of the other patients," a nurse told me. "They won't hurt you. There's a lock on your bedroom door."

"I'm not scared of the other patients," I hissed. "I'm scared of you."

Fear had me in a vice-like grip and though I howled and struggled and tried to fight it off, I was not strong enough. In terrifying hallucinations, sucked into a vortex of despair, I relived those months in the secure unit; my underwear held up for everyone to snigger at, the kebab in the bin, the staff yanking my shoulder behind my back as they shoved my face into the carpet. I could taste the dust and I was choking on it.

"Help!" I yelled. "Somebody get me out of this!"

But there was nobody there. Early in the New Year, I was moved to The Priory, where I spent four weeks receiving therapy. Lucy and Jake visited every regularly and, to my alarm, they told me my final wishes and my goodbye letters were all complete nonsense. My words, so carefully considered at the time, were unintelligible. Lucy, though, had been through my bank statements, and unravelled my gambling addiction.

"Mum, you've got to get help," she told me.

At first, I didn't understand the fuss. I didn't even want help.

"Can you let me out, so that I can go to Aldi?" I'd ask the staff. "I need to buy a bottle of Champagne so I can try to do it properly this time. I'm planning an overdose."

I was so matter of fact. It was as though I was planning a dinner party.

With the correct medication and therapy, my mindset slowly began to change. Even after I was discharged, I had daily therapy, through the early months of 2023. I gave up my job and I lost my home. I went from being a successful, independent, professional, to living in supported accommodation. It was a drastic change and yet possessions had never really interested me. I was beginning to see, in the wider picture, just how lucky I was.

Into the summer of 2023, I was well enough to return to work part-time, as a freelance adviser on child welfare. I moved into a new place in Eastbourne. I had to start all over again, but then, I was used to that. Whilst the circumstances of my breakdown were utterly bizarre, I strongly believe it had to happen. My mental disintegration had been bubbling ever since that first time Dougie chased me round the field at sports day. I finally got the help I should have had as a small child. Conversely, trying to kill myself made me appreciate just how much I wanted to be alive.

* * * *

Thankfully, one year on, I'm pleased to report my life is rather boring again. I am single, free from addiction, and working hard. I enjoy crafts, sewing, flower-arranging and, most of all, spending time with my children and grandchildren.

I will always have hang-ups from my childhood. I can't change what's gone. I have severe scarring, but though it occasionally drags me down, I am learning to hold my head high. I started out life on the at-risk register and I sure as hell won't leave it that way. I've learned that walking around filled with resentment and regret is harmful only to me. It's like drinking poison myself and expecting the enemy to drop dead. I'll never stop fighting; fighting for the child within me, and for all the other kids like me. But I'll never stop smiling either.

I have my family to thank for my happiness. My three granddaughters, aged 13, six and four, are the apples of my eye; little jewels plucked from the smashed glass of my past. Each September, one of my biggest pleasures is buying their school uniforms and school shoes, to make sure they blend in beautifully with all the other kids. I know from bitter experience how important that is. I insist on getting good coats for them, and I also buy their school snacks; organic, of course! Every Christmas, I take them to panto, and on Christmas Eve, they receive a box of goodies. We have holidays, days out and treats. Most importantly, we have love. My grandchildren have everything I always dreamed of as a child, and that is exactly how it should be.

Lucy is a beauty therapist and a busy mum. Jake is a devoted dad and an engineer. In September 2023, Lucy was married in a story-book ceremony on the beach in Cyprus. For me, it was the realisation of my long-held childhood dream. Seeing my beautiful little girl, in her long white dress, with her handsome groom waiting on the sand, was a moment of pure magic. It was a million times better, experienced through my daughter's eyes. My fairytale came true, at last.

An Open Letter to My Mother

DEAR MUM,

How life has changed since I wrote to Dad in my first book, Hackney Child. I had a very different view on my childhood and you as my mum back then. I am sorry the letter hurt you – if I could take the letter back I would. You see, I get now the pain and trauma you have experienced in your life – and instead of anger towards you, I feel admiration. You are one of the strongest people I have ever met. I am so happy you have found peace and to be able to show you that I forgive you. You have been let down and hurt all of your life – it is so beautiful to see you living in peace now. You and dad were a toxic mix, bonded by trauma, but dedicated to each other. There is no time for regret – thank you for trying your best to be my mum

Love, Hope

Acknowledgements

I HAVE so many people to thank for getting me to this point in my life – I hope I don't forget anyone! Forgive me if I do.

First of all, to my beautiful children. I am so deeply proud of the human beings you have grown up to be, I love you with all my heart. To my son and daughter in law, you are so loved in our family. To my grandchildren, thank you for being the incredible little people that you are, love you all. Thank you to my Stevie for being you – I am so happy we found each other.

Rebecca Winfield, my agent. You have believed in me for 10 years, the best agent anyone could wish for.

Jo F, Danielle, Jen, Derek, Ethan and my Sandra, thank you for your love and support over the years, love you all. I am a lucky girl to have so many friends. Cherelle, my Sponsor, love you. Thank you to all at St Jude's. Ann for being a patient and understanding ghost writer – we did it girl!

Thank you to all of my young people who have given me the privilege of your time and stories over the years – you won't know this but I remember all of you and will forever hold you in my heart. Thank you to all the social workers who I have worked with over the years – thank you for giving me your respect and time, you underestimate your importance to children in care, you are incredible role models for them – try to remember this when times are tough.

Finally – to my foster mummy and daddy – I am deeply sad my foster dad is no longer here and will not get to see this book published – you were so proud of me, I miss you so much and am looking after my foster mum.

Other bestselling titles written by Hope Daniels

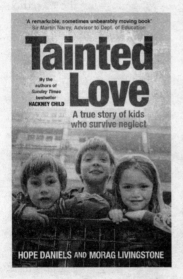

Other bestselling Mirror Books written by Ann Cusack

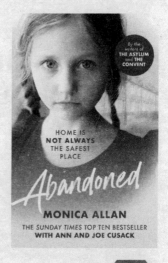